Lifetime

Level 1

Student's Book

Tom Hutchinson

OXFORD

UNIVERSITY PRESS

Oxford University Press
Great Clarendon Street, Oxford OX2 6DP

Oxford New York
Athens Auckland Bangkok Bogotá
Buenos Aires Calcutta Cape Town Chennai
Dar es Salaam Delhi Florence Hong Kong
Istanbul Karachi Kuala Lumpur Madrid
Melbourne Mexico City Mumbai Nairobi
Paris São Paulo Singapore Taipei Tokyo
Toronto Warsaw

and associated companies in
Berlin Ibadan

OXFORD and OXFORD ENGLISH
are trade marks of Oxford University Press

ISBN 019 459047 X   (Student's Book)
ISBN 019 459048 8   (Teacher's Book)

ISBN 019 459043 7   (VHS PAL Cassette)
ISBN 019 459044 5   (VHS SECAM Cassette)
ISBN 019 459045 3   (VHS NTSC Cassette)

© Oxford University Press 1999

Printed in Hong Kong

Stills photography:
Rob Judges

Illustrations:
Moira Willis
Paul Dickinson

The publishers would like to thank the following for permission to
reproduce photographs:
Kos Picture Source Ltd
Robert Harding Picture Library

The author would like to thank everyone at OUP who has
contributed their skills and expertise to the making of the
Lifetime video and Student's Book, particularly Rob Maidment
(Producer and Director), Martyn Hobbs (Script editor), Louis
Harrison (Editor) and Rob Hancock (Designer)

For Eunice

EPISODE 1

Julia's first day

1

Watch the whole of Episode 1. Write the names and the jobs in the correct places.

Gary	Drake	the Managing Director
Colin	Bond	a reporter
Sandra	Barnes	a producer
Julia	Fenton	a trainee
Martha	McKay	a newsreader
Rebecca		a personal assistant
Ted		
Tim		

a

Name _ _ _ _ _ Harris _ _ _ _ _

Job _ _ the Security Officer _ _

b

Name _ _ _ _ _ _ _ _ _ _ _ _ _

Job _ _ _ _ _ _ _ _ _ _ _ _ _

c

Name _ _ _ _ _ _ _ _ _ _ _ _ _

Job _ _ _ _ _ _ _ _ _ _ _ _ _

d

Name _ _ _ _ _ _ _ _ _ _ _ _ _

e

Name _ _ _ _ _ _ _ _ _ _ _ _ _

Job _ _ _ _ _ _ _ _ _ _ _ _ _

f

Name _ _ _ _ _ _ _ _ _ _ _ _ _

Job _ _ _ _ _ _ _ _ _ _ _ _ _

g

Name _ _ _ _ _ Drake _ _ _ _ _

h

Name _ _ _ _ _ _ _ _ _ _ _ _ _

Job _ _ _ _ _ _ _ _ _ _ _ _ _

i

Name _ _ Sean Casey _ _ _

Job _ _ a Cameraman _ _

j

Name _ _ Frederick Mills _ _

Job _ _ _ _ _ _ _ _ _ _ _ _ _

4

B

1

Rewind to the beginning. Watch to JULIA: *Here you are*. Number the pictures in the correct order.

a

b

c

d

e

f

5

g

h

2

Watch again. Which times do you hear?

a

b

c

d

e

3

Watch again. Who says each thing? Match them to the names.

Good morning.	
Here is the news.	
Look at the time.	Sandra
Coming.	Colin
Is this OK?	Julia
Lovely, dear.	Gary
Thanks, Mum. Bye, Dad.	
It's her first day today.	
What?	

C

1

Rewind to the beginning and watch to JULIA: *Thank you.* **Tick the correct answers.**

1 How much is the taxi fare?
- £4.50
- £5.00
- £5.50

2 Who is talking on a mobile phone?
- Rebecca
- Gary
- Tim

3 Who does Julia ask for?
- Martha
- Frederick
- Rebecca

4 What is the extension number?
- 4985
- 5894
- 5498

5 Where does Ted say Julia is?
- at the entrance
- at the Front Desk
- at Reception

6 What is the room number?
- 12
- 20
- 27

7 Which floor is it on?
- the first floor
- the second floor
- the third floor

6

D

1

Watch to MARTHA: *Come on, then, Julia.* **Answer the questions.**

1 Who is on the phone?
2 What is the name of the TV company?
3 Where is Frederick?

2

Watch again. Rebecca makes a file card for Ms Fossett. Complete it.

Name: **Ms Angela Fossett**

Address: ....

....

....
                                    Watlington
....

Postcode: ....

Tel. No.: ....

3

Watch again. Match the halves of the expressions.

1	And what's	a	then, Julia.
2	How do you	b	meet you.
3	Can you	c	personal assistant, Rebecca Bond.
4	Welcome to	d	spell *Tindall*?
5	No, don't	e	see.
6	This is my	f	in?
7	Pleased to	g	Apex TV.
8	Come and meet	h	your address?
9	Is Frederick	i	come in.
10	Oh, I	j	repeat that, please?
11	Come on	k	some of the people in the newsroom.

E

1a

Watch to GARY: *She's very pretty.* **Complete what Julia says.**

name
Julie.
.

1b

Why does she say it?

2

Watch again. Complete the dialogues.

1

MARTHA: _____ *Tim Barnes* _____
there. _____ *a reporter.*

2

MARTHA: *Tim,* _____ *is Julia.* _____
our new trainee.

3

TIM: _____ *is a very interesting story, Martha.*
Look at _____ .

MARTHA: *Tell* _____ *about it* _____
afternoon. OK?

4

GARY: *Who's* _____ *young woman with*
Martha and Sean?

TIM: _____ *name's Julia. She's a new trainee.*

GARY: _____ *very pretty.*

3

Watch again. Put the dialogue in the correct order.

	Oh, right.		*Julia.*
	What?		*My name isn't Julie. It's Julia.*
	Right. Thank you .	ı	*See you around, Julia.*
	Don't mention it.		*And address has got two Ds.*
	Sorry?		*Address is A, double D.*

F

1

Watch to MARTHA: *Yes.* **Which buttons does Martha press for Julia's drink?**

2

Watch again. Look at the picture and answer the questions.

1 What is Gary saying?
   a *You're Julia, aren't you?*
   b *Pleased to meet you. I'm Gary.*
   c *I'm a newsreader.*
   d *I must be off.*

2 What do his gesture and facial expression mean?

3 Why does his smile suddenly disappear?

4 What does the scene tell us about Gary's personality?

G

1

Watch to the end. Answer the questions.

1 Where is Julia?

2 Who is she talking to?

3 Who is on the TV?

4 Where is the person?

2

Watch again. What does Julia say about the person on the TV?

He's great.

He's very friendly.

He isn't very friendly.

He isn't very nice.

He's very nice.

 Watch the whole of Episode 1 again. ◄◄

7

Exercises

1

Look at the pictures on page 4. Introduce the people.

Example

> This is Julia Drake. She's a trainee.

> This is Tim Barnes. He's ...

2

Say these prices.

Example

> four pounds fifty

> twenty-three pence (twenty-three p)

£4.50   23p   £12.30

£6.99   £10.49

60p

12p   £2.16

75p   £3.80

3a

Complete the dialogue.

A: _____ morning. _____ I help
   _____ ?

B: Yes, Martha McKay, _____

A: Mrs McKay is _____ room 12.
   _____ on the _____ floor.
   _____ lifts are _____ there.

B: _____ you.

3b

Make dialogues for these cues. (See *Culture note*, p10.)

1   Jack Hall / Mr / 32 / third floor
2   Olivia West / Miss / 17 / first floor
3   Tom Summers / Mr / 20 / second floor
4   Judy Byng / Ms / 38 / third floor
5   Sally Hamm / Mrs / 11 / first floor

4a

Put the conversation in the correct order.

> I'm fine, thanks. And you?
>
> Good morning, Tim. How are you?
>
> Fine, thanks.
>
> Morning, Ted.

4b

Go round and greet some people in your class.

5a

Complete the dialogue with the expressions.

> And your telephone number?
> Thank you. And what's the postcode?
> How do you spell Tindall, please?
> Thank you, Ms Fossett. Goodbye.
> What's your name, please?
> Can you repeat that, please?
> And what's your address?

REBECCA: _____

MS FOSSETT: *It's Angela Fossett.*

REBECCA: _____

MS FOSSETT: *94 Tindall Street.*

REBECCA: _____

MS FOSSETT: *It's T - I - N - D - A double L.*

REBECCA: _____

MS FOSSETT: *KT9 8NB.*

REBECCA: _____

MS FOSSETT: *Yes, of course. It's KT9 8NB.*

REBECCA: _____

MS FOSSETT: *It's 01372 89531.*

REBECCA: _____

MS FOSSETT: *Goodbye.*

8

5b

Make new dialogues for this information.

Mr Paul Collins
59 Arron Road
Oxford
OX5 7JD
01865 446092

Mrs Helen Box
22 Beecham Street
Cambridge
CB2 4KT
01223 298431

6

Complete the dialogues with the words.

woman   he's   she's   his   man   her

Ted

A: Who's that .... over there?

B: .... name's Ted. .... the Security Officer.

Martha

A: Who's that .... over there?

B: .... name's Martha. .... a producer.

7

Ask people in the class what they would like to drink.

Examples

	A	B

1

Tea or coffee?

Tea, please.

Milk and sugar?

Just milk, please. No sugar.

Here you are.

2

Tea or coffee?

Coffee, please.

Black or white?

Black with sugar, please.

Here you are.

Role play

Work in a group of five. Write and act a play to fit this scenario.

Student A: You are a new trainee at Apex TV. Go to Reception and ask for Martha.

Student B: You are the Security Officer. Deal with Student A.

Student C: You are Martha. Welcome Student A. Offer him / her a drink. Take him / her into the newsroom to introduce him / her to Student D.

Student D: Martha introduces Student A to you. Ask Student A some questions.

Student E: You see Student A on his / her own. Introduce yourself to Student A.

9

Language in use

1 Responses

Match the items in A with the items in B.

A		B	
1	How do you do?	a	Don't mention it.
2	Come on. It's seven o'clock.	b	I'm fine, thanks. And you?
3	That's two pounds ninety, please.	c	I'm a reporter.
4	It's my first day today.	d	Here you are.
5	Excuse me.	e	Thank you very much.
6	How are you?	f	Sorry.
7	Hello, I'm Julia.	g	Yes. Bye.
8	See you.	h	Coming.
9	What do you do?	i	Well, good luck.
10	Thank you.	j	Welcome to Apex TV, Julia.
11	Frederick isn't here.	k	Oh, I see.
12	Here you are.	l	Pleased to meet you.

2 Meeting people

Number the dialogue in the correct order.

	I'm a cameraman.	**1**	Hello. My name's Peter.
	Well, I must be off. See you around.		Nice to meet you, Karen. What do you do?
	Pleased to meet you, Peter. I'm Karen.		I'm a secretary. And you?
	Yes. Bye.		

3 Useful expressions

Delete the incorrect expression.

1   Here is the news.
    ~~Here are the news.~~

2   See the time.
    Look at the time.

3   Can I help you?
    I can help you?

4   Hi. I'm at home.
    Hi. I'm home.

5   Tell all about it.
    Tell me all about it.

6   How's your new job?
    How's your new work?

4 Agreeing

Which expressions are appropriate ways of agreeing? Delete the inappropriate ways.

5 Greeting and leaving

Write these expressions in the correct column.

Good morning.   Bye.   Morning.   See you.   Hello.
Hi.   See you around.   Good evening.   Goodbye.
Good afternoon.   Goodnight.   See you later.

Greeting	Leaving

Culture note: titles

MALE
We use *Mr* /mɪstə/ for men.
We use *Master* for boys.

FEMALE
We can use *Ms* for any woman.
We use *Mrs* /mɪsɪz/ for a married woman.
We use *Miss* for an unmarried woman of any age or for a girl.

Note: In work situations, people normally use first names: Martha, Tim, etc.

Grammar summary

to be

Positive statements

I	'm (am)	a new trainee.
He She It	's (is)	
You We They	're (are)	reporters.

Negative statements

I	'm not ('m not)	in the office.
He She It	isn't (is not)	
You We They	aren't (are not)	

Questions

Am	I	a newsreader?
Is	he she it	
Are	we you they	in the newsroom?

Short answers

Yes,	I am. he is. she is.	No,	I'm not. he isn't. she isn't.

Numbers 1 – 100

1	one	18	eighteen
2	two	19	nineteen
3	three	20	twenty
4	four	21	twenty-one
5	five	22	twenty-two
6	six	23	twenty-three
7	seven	30	thirty
8	eight	40	forty
9	nine	50	fifty
10	ten	60	sixty
11	eleven	70	seventy
12	twelve	80	eighty
13	thirteen	90	ninety
14	fourteen	100	a hundred
15	fifteen		
16	sixteen		
17	seventeen		

this / that, these / those

Singular

This is Rebecca.

That's Gary.

Plural

These letters are important.

Those computers are new.

We use *this* and *these* for people and things close to us.

We use *that* and *those* for people and things that are further away.

Imperatives

We make the imperative using the stem form of the verb. We use *don't* + the stem form for negatives.

Come in.	Don't come in.
Look.	Don't look.

a / an, the

We use *a* or *an* with jobs.

*She's **a** new trainee.*

*I'm **an** accountant.*

If there is only one position in a company we use *the*.

*He's **the** Managing Director.*

Possessive adjectives

This is	my your his her its our your their	telephone number. first day.

The possessive adjectives *his* and *her* agree with the possessor, not the thing that is possessed.

*This is **Tim** at **his** desk.*

*This is **Rebecca** at **her** desk.*

11

EPISODE 2

And ... action!

While you watch

1a

Before you watch, read this greeting. Who do you think says it?

> *Good morning, Julia. How nice to see you.*

1b

Watch to: *How nice to see you.* **Check your idea. Why does he / she say it?**

2

Watch again. Answer the questions.

1   Tim is talking to someone on the phone. What is his / her name?

2   Who do you think he / she is?

3   What is the problem?

4   How does Tim feel about the conversation?

1

Watch to TIM: *Martha, Can I have a word?* **Answer the questions.**

1   What are Rebecca and Martha doing?

2   What day is it?

3   Where does Frederick have to go?

2a

Watch again. What does Martha have to do?

- [ ] read the News
- [x] finish the Videocom report
- [ ] have a meeting with Floyd and Hank
- [ ] meet some visitors from Spain
- [ ] go to the Birmingham conference
- [ ] have a meeting with Frederick
- [ ] go to Paris with Frederick
- [ ] do the food programme
- [ ] go to the dentist's

2b

Complete Martha's diary. Write the correct times.

August
Monday
Tuesday
Wednesday
Thursday

12

C

Watch to MARTHA: *See you later.* **Answer the questions.**

1   What is Tim's problem?
2   What does Julia suggest?
3   How does Tim feel about it?
4   What does Martha think about it?
5   What is the result?

2

Watch again. Match the halves of the sentences.

1

Can I	is it?
Yes, Tim. What	an assistant for this afternoon.
I haven't got	have a word?

2

Chloe's	busy.
Gita's	on holiday.
And everybody else is	away.

3

But I have to	do it?
Can I	an idea.
That's	have an assistant.

4

She hasn't	nobody else.
She has	got the experience.
And there's	to learn.

D

Watch to TIM: *... sharp.* **Tick the correct endings.**

1   The company's name is …
     Western Windows.
     Wonderful Windows.
     Walker's Windows.
2   The windows cost …
     £400.
     £500.
     £600.
3   The man's name is …
     Bill Walker.
     Harry Horton.
     Carl Stalker.
4   He's …
     the Managing Director.
     the manager.
     one of the directors.
5   The problem is …
     the windows are no good.
     the company hasn't got any money.
     the customers haven't got their windows.
6   They have to leave at …
     12.40.
     1.20.
     1.30.

2

Watch again. Complete the advertisement.

3

What is Tim giving Julia?

13

1

Watch to TIM: *When you see him, call me.*
Answer the questions.

1   Where do you think Tim, Sean and Julia are?

2   How does Tim react to Sean's news about Jason?

3   What do Julia and Sean talk about?

4   What does Tim give to Julia?

5   What does she have to do?

2

Watch again. Are these statements true (T) or false (F)?

1   Sean has got three children.

2   His son's name is Jason.

3   He has got a daughter called Kylie.

4   She's fifteen.

5   Jason is sixteen.

6   Kylie is in trouble at school.

7   Sean's wife's name is Karen.

8   Stalker's car is a white Mercedes.

9   He isn't very tall.

10   Stalker's got short, dark hair.

14

1

Watch to JULIA: *Are you all right, Sean?*
Number the pictures in the correct order.

a

b

c

d

e

f

g

h

2

Watch again. Match Stalker's responses to Tim's questions.

1 I'm from Apex TV. Can I ask you some questions?

2 Where is your customers' money, Mr Stalker?

3 You and your wife have got a very big house and an expensive car, but your customers have got nothing. Where is their money, Mr Stalker?

4 Where's the money, Mr Stalker?

a Clear off!

b I've got nothing to say.

c What the … ? No, you can't.

d Look. Go away and switch that thing off.

G

1a

Watch to the end of Episode 2. Answer the questions.

1 What's the time?
2 Why does Tim make a phone call?
3 Who does he speak to?
4 Where do Sean, Tim and Julia go?

1b

Look at this picture. Answer the questions.

1 What is the woman's name?
2 Who is she?
3 What is she saying? Write it in the speech bubble.

15

2

Watch again. What do you think Julia is going to say? Why?

Are you and Rebecca … ?

H

1

How observant are you? What are the colours and registration numbers of these cars?

1 Stalker's car
2 the first car that Julia reported
3 Sean's car
4 Tim's car

▲ Watch the whole of Episode 2 again. Check your ideas. ◄◄

Exercises

1a

Say these times.

Example

It's half past seven.

1b

Now give the times in digital form.

Example

It's seven thirty.

2

Write *in*, *on*, *at* or / if there is no preposition.

1   in   the morning

2   _____   10.20

3   _____   tomorrow

4   _____   Monday

5   _____   Saturday afternoon

6   _____   this afternoon

7   _____   half past nine

8   _____   the afternoon

9   _____   Wednesday

10 _____   this morning

11 _____   the evening

12 _____   9.30   _____   Wednesday evening

13 _____   quarter to three

14 _____   today

15 _____   this evening

3

Write in the prepositions.

1   You've got a meeting _____ Frederick.

2   I have to go _____ London.

3   New windows _____ just £500.

4   I've got an appointment _____ the dentist's.

5   Frederick is the Managing Director _____ Apex TV.

6   Is Chloe _____ holiday?

7   This story is _____ a guy called Stalker.

8   Tim hasn't got an assistant _____ his report.

9   Martha's _____ a conference _____ Wednesday.

10 Can I take a look _____ the diary for today?

4a

Look at Martha's diary on page 12. What does she have to do this week?

Example

On Monday morning she has to do the food programme.

4b

Look at Julia's list of jobs for Monday. What does she say?

Example

I have to read the letters from Stalker's customers.

1 Read the letters from Stalker's customers.

2 Help martha on the food programme.

3 Go to the bank.

4 Get a sandwich for lunch.

5 Phone Hank's secretary.

6 Meet Tim at 1.30.

5

Look at Sean's family tree and describe the relationships.

Example

Jason / Sean and Sharon

Jason is Sean and Sharon's son.

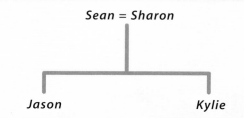

Sean = Sharon

Jason   Kylie

1   Sean / Sharon

2   Jason / Kylie

3   Sean / Kylie

4   Kylie / Sean and Sharon

5   Kylie and Jason / Sean and Sharon

6   Sharon / Sean

7   Sean and Sharon / Jason

8   Sharon / Kylie

9   Kylie / Jason

6

Complete the sentences with *have got*,
has got, *haven't got* **or** *hasn't got*.

1 Stalker _____ a big car.

2 Sean and Sharon _____ two children.

3 Julia _____ a car.

4 Stalker's customers _____ their windows.

5 Stalker and his wife _____ an expensive house.

6 Tim _____ a girlfriend.

7 Martha _____ a personal assistant.

8 Rebecca and Ellie _____ a flat.

7

Put the words in brackets into the correct order to complete the dialogues.

1

MR PARKER: *Can I see* Mrs McKay, please?
(see / can / I)

REBECCA: _____ an appointment?

(got / you / have)

MR PARKER: _____ . (haven't / I / no)

REBECCA: I'm sorry, but _____ you today.
(can't / she / see)

MR PARKER: Oh, I see. Well, _____ an appointment for tomorrow, then?
(I / can / make)

REBECCA: _____ at 10.30? (come / you / can)

MR PARKER: Yes, that's fine.

REBECCA: _____ me your name then, please?
(you / can / give)

MR PARKER: Yes, it's John Parker.

2

FLOYD: _____ an assistant for tomorrow.
(haven't / I / got)

MARTHA: What about Julia? _____ anything to do tomorrow. (got / she / hasn't)

FLOYD: _____ the experience?
(got / she / has)

MARTHA: No, but I'm sure _____ it.
(she / do / can)

FLOYD: _____ ? (drive / can / she)

MARTHA: _____ . (can / yes / she)

FLOYD: _____ a car? (has / she / got)

MARTHA: _____ . (hasn't / she / no)

FLOYD: Oh, that's OK. _____ my car.
(she / use / can)

8a

Complete the description of Stalker.

A: *What does Stalker look like?*

B: *He's _____ tall.*
He's got _____
dark hair and brown
_____ .

8b

Describe these people.

Julia   Sean

Rebecca   Tim

Gary   Martha

Work in a group of three. Write and act a play to fit this scenario.

Student A is a politician, Student B is his / her personal assistant, Student C is a reporter.

Some money has disappeared. The politician is discussing his / her diary for the week with his / her personal assistant.
The reporter arrives. He / she wants to interview the politician about the money.
The politician doesn't want to answer any questions.

Language in use

1 Describing people

Put the words in the correct places.

blue   look   hair   beard   slim   very   fair   long

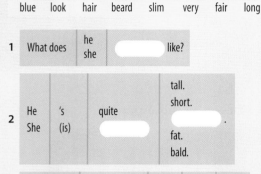

| 1 | What does | he
she | [____] | like? |

| 2 | He
She | 's
(is) | quite | [____] | tall.
short.
[____].
fat.
bald. |

| 3 | What colour | [____]
eyes | has | he
she | got? |

| 4 | He
She | 's got
(has got) | blond
short
[____]
medium length
black | brown
dark | hair and | [____]
green
brown | eyes. |

| 5 | He
She | 's got
(has got) | a moustache.
a [____].
glasses. |

2 Requests and suggestions

Match the halves of the sentences.

Can we take a look	a drink?
Can I have	some questions?
Can I ask you	the programme for me, please?
Can you video	at the diary?
How about	the usual place?
See you at	a word, please?

3 Responses

Make dialogues. Choose appropriate responses from the list below to the requests and suggestions in Exercise 2.

Example

A: Can we take a look at the diary?

B: Yes, OK. or I'm sorry. I haven't got time.

Yes. What is it?

Yes, OK.

OK. Let's go.

That's an idea.

Yes. See you there.

I'm sorry. I haven't got time.

I've got nothing to say.

Just a minute. I have to make a phone call.

4 Useful expressions

Look at the transcript for Episode 2. Find suitable expressions to fill the speech bubbles.

Grammar summary

have got
Positive statements

I You We They	've got (have got)	a blue car. short dark hair. a meeting.
He She It	's got (has got)	

Negative statements

I We They	haven't got (have not got)	time. a car. an assistant.
He She It	hasn't got (has not got)	

Questions

Have	I you we they	got	an appointment ? time ?
Has	he she it		

Short answers

Yes,	I have. he has. she has.	No,	I haven't. he hasn't. she hasn't.

can / can't
We use *can* to talk about ability.

I You He She It We They	can can't (cannot)	drive a car. use a computer. speak German.

We use *can / can't* to make requests.

***Can** I take tommorrow off ?*

***Can** you video the football match for me?*

We also use *can / can't* to make offers.

***Can** I help you?*

***Can** I do it for you?*

have to
We use *have to* to talk about obligation.

I You We They	have to	finish this report. learn English.
He She It	has to	

Note: *have / has to* is always used in the full form. There is no short answer.

Days of the week
Monday, Tuesday, Wednesday, Thursday, Friday, Saturday, Sunday

Telling the time

It's twelve o'clock.
or It's twelve o'clock.

It's five past three.
or It's three-oh-five.

It's ten past nine.
or It's nine ten

It's quarter past four.
or It's four fifteen.

It's twenty past two.
or It's two twenty.

It's twenty-five past six.
or It's six twenty-five.

It's half past two.
or It's two-thirty.

It's twenty-five to eleven.
or It's ten thirty-five.

It's twenty to four.
or It's three forty.

It's a quarter to eleven.
or It's ten forty-five.

It's ten to seven.
or It's six fifty.

It's five to three.
or It's two fifty-five.

Prepositions – *in, at, on*

We use *in* for

- parts of the day

***in** the morning,* ***in** the evening*

- years, months and seasons

***in** 1998,* ***in** September,* ***in** summer*

We use *at* for

- exact times

***at** 10 o'clock,* ***at** 12.30*

- weekends and public holidays

***at** the weekend,* ***at** Christmas*

We use *on* for

- particular days

***on** Saturday,* ***on** 21 January,* ***on** Christmas day*

EPISODE 3

The Joker

A

1

Watch until the telephone rings. Look at the picture and answer the questions.

1 What is Gary reading?
2 Whose desk is it?
3 What does the desk tell us about his / her personality?

2

Watch again. Number the events in the correct order.

	He picks up the magazine and looks at it.
	She has a drink of coffee.
	Gary knocks on Martha's door.
	She puts the letters in a tray.
	She answers the phone.
	Rebecca comes back with a cup of coffee.
	He looks at the diary on Rebecca's desk.
1	Rebecca comes in with the morning post.
	The phone rings.
	She goes to get a cup of coffee.
	Gary leaves.
	She puts the magazine on her desk.
	She picks up the magazine and looks at it.
	She sits down.

B

1

Watch to REBECCA: *Well, yes, of course.*
Answer the questions.

1 Who is Angus Moon?
2 Why is he phoning Rebecca?
3 How does he know about her?
4 What is a PA?
5 What does Angus Moon want to do now?
6 How does Rebecca feel about the interview?

20

C

1

Watch to **REBECCA:** *Well, I don't think it's funny.*
Why does she say this?

2

Watch again. Are these statements true
(T) or false (F)?

1   Rebecca gets up at quarter past seven. ☐
2   She has her breakfast before she
    gets dressed. ☐
3   She has a glass of grapefruit juice
    for breakfast. ☐
4   She always has the same things
    for breakfast. ☐
5   She drinks coffee in the morning. ☐
6   She doesn't go to the gym on
    Wednesdays. ☐
7   She doesn't like cooking. ☐

3a

Tick the things that Rebecca mentions.

1   In the morning she …
    ☐ gets up.   ☐ has breakfast.
    ☐ cleans her teeth.   ☐ has a shower.
    ☐ washes her hair.   ☐ listens to the radio.
    ☐ gets dressed.

2   For breakfast she has …
    ☐ a glass of orange juice.   ☐ bacon and eggs.
    ☐ a grapefruit.   ☐ toast.
    ☐ cereal.   ☐ coffee.
    ☐ jam.   ☐ marmalade.
    ☐ butter.   ☐ cheese.

3   In her free time she …
    ☐ goes to the gym.   ☐ plays badminton.
    ☐ sings.   ☐ goes to a dance class.
    ☐ rides a horse.   ☐ goes swimming.

4   She likes …
    ☐ skiing.   ☐ dancing.
    ☐ painting.   ☐ cooking.
    ☐ going to parties.   ☐ shopping.

3b

Watch again. Check your answers.

4a

Complete what Gary says.

You're very
_____ .

OK, Rebecca.
Thank you
_____ .

Hey. It's
only _____ .

4b

Write Rebecca's replies in the speech
bubbles.

D

1

Watch until Gary appears. Answer the
questions.

1   What is the programme?
2   What does Martha always do?
3   Why does Rebecca come in?
4   Where is Frederick?
5   How long is the break?
6   Where is Gary?
7   What do you think Gary is going to do?

21

1

Watch to MARTHA: *It's time to try it.* **Which of these does Gary use? Tick the correct items. What does he do with them?**

    pepper

    salt

    whisky

    vinegar

    chilli powder

    an insect

    sugar

2a

What do you think happens next?

2b

Watch to MARTHA: *… Bye.* **Check your ideas.**

3

Watch from MARTHA: *It's time to try it.* **to MARTHA:** *… Bye.* **again. Label the things in the pictures.**

4

Watch again. Match the halves of the sentences.

1	Is everything		a	to try it.
2	Yes, I think		b	for this week.
3	Do you want		c	want to.
4	But, um, can I		d	make a change today?
5	If you		e	wait to taste it.
6	It's time		f	wonderful, Gary?
7	Why don't we		g	ready?
8	Would you like to		h	as much as Gary.
9	I bet you can't		i	watch?
10	Here. Try the		j	try this delicious meal, Gary?
11	Isn't that		k	about this soup?
12	Now what		l	home-made lemonade first.
13	Come on,		m	so.
14	Well, that's it		n	try it?
15	I hope you enjoy your summer lunch		o	a big spoonful.

5

Watch again. Answer the questions.

1   Why did Gary think his joke would work?

2   How do you think Martha realized?

22

F

1

Watch to JULIA: *Who's Ellie?* **Tick the drinks that people ask for.**

- tea
- white wine
- beer
- coffee
- mineral water
- lemonade

2a

Watch again. Complete the dialogue.

_____ : OK. What would you _____ ?

_____ : I'll have a _____ , please.

_____ : _____ , too.

_____ : Home-made _____ for _____ , please, Gary.

_____ : Very _____ .

_____ : Just a _____ , Gary. Just a _____ .

_____ : I'll have a _____ . I have to _____ .

_____ : Ice and _____ ?

_____ : Yes, please. Oh, I must give _____ a _____ .

2b

Who says each thing?

G

1

Watch to the end. Who is this?

2

Watch again. Are these statements true (T) or false (F)?

1 Rebecca and Julia are talking about Martha.

2 Julia thinks Rebecca is Tim's girlfriend.

3 Ellie is Tim's sister.

4 Ellie is Rebecca's flatmate.

5 Tim lives next door to Rebecca.

6 Ellie works for an airline.

7 She travels a lot.

8 She doesn't work normal hours.

23

3

Watch again. Answer the questions.

1 Why does Julia think Rebecca is Tim's girlfriend?

2 Why is there no reply?

3 What do you think is happening?

▲ Watch the whole of Episode 3 again. ◀◀

Exercises

1

Martin, the editor of the Apex TV staff magazine wants to write an article about Julia, so that people will know something about her. Here he is interviewing Julia. Write Martin's questions. Use the cues.

Example

MARTIN: **What do you do?** *(What / do)*

JULIA: *I'm a trainee.*

MARTIN: _____

    (Who / work / with)

JULIA: *I work with Martha McKay, on the food programme mostly.*

MARTIN: _____ *(like / cooking)*

JULIA: *No. I like food, but I don't really like cooking.*

MARTIN: _____

    (Where / live)

JULIA: *I live with my parents.*

MARTIN: _____

    (How / travel / to work)

JULIA: *I come by train.*

MARTIN: _____

    (What time / have to / get up?)

JULIA: *At half past six.*

MARTIN: _____

    (like / getting up early)

JULIA: *No, I don't.*

MARTIN: _____

    (What / do / in your free time)

JULIA: *I go to the theatre and the cinema. I watch television and I read a lot, too.*

MARTIN: _____

    (What / read)

JULIA: *Mostly novels.*

MARTIN: _____

    (play / any sports)

JULIA: *No, I don't.*

MARTIN: _____

    (What / enjoy / most)

JULIA: *Oh, going to parties, I think.*

2

Complete Martin's article about Julia.

new faces

Julia Drake

Julia Drake is a new trainee at Apex TV. She _____ with Martha McKay, mostly on the food programme. Julia says that she _____ food, but she _____ cooking. Julia _____ with her parents and she _____ to work by train. She _____ to get up at half past six, but she _____ getting up early. In her free time she _____ to the theatre and the cinema, she _____ television and she _____ a lot, too. She _____ any sports. Most of all she _____ going to parties.

3

Interview a partner and write an article about him / her for the staff magazine.

4

Say whether you like doing these things or not.

Example

I like playing football. / I don't like playing football.

1   playing football
2   getting up early
3   travelling by train
4   watching sports programmes on TV
5   cooking
6   going to parties
7   trying new kinds of food
8   reading novels
9   playing jokes on people
10 waiting

24

5

Rewrite these sentences about Gary using the words in brackets.

Example

Gary drinks tea in the morning. (always)

Gary always drinks tea in the morning.

1 He doesn't have any breakfast. (usually)

2 He gets up very early. (sometimes)

3 He's friendly. (always)

4 He plays jokes on people. (often)

5 He drives to work. (normally)

6 He works in the studio. (always)

7 He doesn't read magazines. (often)

8 He's quite organized. (normally)

9 He wears smart clothes. (always)

10 He's on TV every day. (usually)

11 He goes to the gym. (never)

6

Describe the things in the pictures. Use these words.

spoonful   cup   glass   bowl   packet   bottle   box   slice

Example

two cups of tea

7

Tim wants to do a report on a man called Jack Hinchcliffe. Here he's talking about him to Kate, a researcher at Apex TV. Use these verbs to complete Tim's questions. Some of the verbs are used more than once.

come   go out   drive   go   live   work   look

Example

TIM: *What does he look like?*

KATE: *He's quite short and bald.*

TIM: *Where* ?

KATE: *He lives in a big house in Newlands Road.*

TIM: *on his own?*

KATE: *No. He lives with his wife.*

TIM: *What kind of car* ?

KATE: *A green BMW.*

TIM: *Where* ?

KATE: *He works somewhere in London.*

TIM: *What time to work?*

KATE: *At half past seven.*

TIM: *into London?*

KATE: *No, he doesn't. He goes by train.*

TIM: *home at the same time every day?*

KATE: *Yes, he always gets the 5.45 train.*

TIM: *in the evening?*

KATE: *No. He usually stays at home.*

TIM: *Thanks, Kate.*

Role play

Work in a group of three. Write and act a play to fit this scenario.

Students A, B and C work together. They go to the pub for a drink.

Student A offers to buy the drinks. Students B and C tell him / her what they want. While Student A orders the drinks, Student B goes to make a phone call.

Students A and C sit down with their drinks. Student B phones Student C to try and play a joke on him / her. After a while Student C realizes who it is. Students A and C then play a joke on Student B.

Language in use

1 Suggesting and accepting / refusing

Make dialogues with the expressions.

Why don't we	go for a drink?
Would you like to	try this food?
Do you want to	watch the news?
Shall we	go swimming?

Yes, please.
No, thank you.

2 Useful expressions

Look at the transcript on page 61. Find expressions which mean the same as these.

Example

1 This is Rebecca Bond.
   Rebecca Bond speaking.

2 I know Martha very well.

3 Have you got time to do something now?

4 I'm sure you want to taste it.

5 That's the end.

6 I must phone Ellie.

7 Nobody is answering the phone.

3 Responses

Make dialogues with the sentences below. Choose suitable responses from this list.

I think so.	Me, too.	If you want to.

Example

1 Can I watch the News?
   If you want to.

2 Are you ready?

3 I'll have an orange juice, please.

4 I'd like to take a holiday.

5 Can I use your phone?

6 Is Martha in her office?

7 Why don't we go for a drink?

8 Has Sean got two children?

9 I like skiing.

10 Is that it for today?

4 In a pub

Number this dialogue in the correct order.

_____ Yes, please.

_____ Me, too.

_____ I'll have a glass of wine, please.

_____ Ice and lemon?

_____ So that's two glasses of wine, a mineral water with ice and lemon and a pint of lager, please.

_____ What would you like?

_____ And I'll have a mineral water, please.

Culture note: drinks

The normal places to drink in Britain are pubs, wine bars and cafés. Most of them serve tea and coffee and food as well as alcoholic drinks.

Normally, one person offers to buy a drink for everyone in the group. This is called buying a round. The next time, another member of the group buys the round.

In pubs and wine bars you have to go to the bar to order your drinks and you pay for them immediately. In cafés there is usually a waiter or waitress to bring your drinks.

Most places have several kinds of beer, so you can't just order *beer*, you have to say what kind of beer you want. You can get beer in bottles or on draught (i.e. from a barrel). You normally buy a *pint* of draught beer. The two most popular kinds of beer are *bitter*, a traditional British beer, and *lager*, which is similar to the beer in many other countries.

26

Grammar summary

The Present simple tense

We use the Present simple tense to talk about

- routines and habits

*I **get up** at seven every day.*

*She **goes** to her dance class on Thursday.*

- things that are always true

*He **comes** from England.*

Positive statements

I We You They	work live	
He She It	works lives	here. in London.

Negative statements

I We You They	don't (do not)	
He She It	doesn't (does not)	work in London. live here.

Questions

Do	I we you they	
Does	he she it	work in London? live here?

Short answers

Yes,	I do. he does. she does.	No,	I don't. he doesn't. she doesn't.

Wh– questions

To make *Wh–* questions, we use the normal question form and a question word.

***What** do you have for breakfast?*

***Where** does she work?*

***How** do you travel to work?*

like + – ing

Like and other verbs which describe feelings are usually followed by *-ing*.

I	like	
He	enjoys	dancing. going to parties. cooking.
She	dislikes	

Adverbs of frequency

We use adverbs of frequency with the Present simple tense to say how often we do something.

100%	always usually often sometimes hardly ever
0%	never

The adverb of frequency usually goes

– before a normal verb

*Rebecca **always** gets up at seven o'clock.*

– after the verb *to be* or an auxiliary verb

*She's **often** late.*

*We can **usually** find a taxi.*

some / any

We use *some* in positive statements.

*We need **some** oranges.*

*I always have **some** bread with the soup.*

We use *any* with negative statements and questions.

*There isn't **any** ice in the lemonade.*

*Is there **any** salt?*

Countable and uncountable nouns

Some nouns are countable. They have got a plural form.

a grapefruit	two grapefruits
an egg	three eggs
a tomato	some tomatoes

Some nouns are uncountable. They haven't got a plural form.

salt	~~salts~~
water	~~waters~~
beef	~~beefs~~

With uncountable nouns we can't use *a* or *an* – we use *some* or *any*.

We also use the following expressions with uncountable nouns.

a slice of
a bowl of
a glass of
a cup of

27

Happy birthday

1

Look at the pictures. Answer the questions.

1 Who is in each picture?

2 Where are they?

3 What do you think is happening?

2

Watch the whole of Episode 4. Number the pictures in the correct order.

B

1

Watch to JULIA: ... *a flat in town.* **Are these statements true (T) or false (F)?**

1 Tim was in bed at five o'clock this morning.

2 There was an accident at the station.

3 There weren't any trains for six hours.

4 It's the third of October.

5 It's Ellie's birthday.

6 Tim has got her a card and a present.

7 Julia is late for work.

8 She isn't often late.

2

Answer the questions.

1 Where does Tim go?

2 What does Julia decide to do?

3a

Watch again. Complete the expressions.

1

⬭ : And what do you know about the fourth of October?

TIM: *It's* ⬭ ?

2

⬭ : Good ⬭ , Julia.

JULIA: *I know. I'm sorry.*

3

JULIA: *Is Martha annoyed?*

⬭ : *Well, she* ⬭ .

3b

Who says each thing?

3c

Match the meanings to the expressions in the dialogues.

You're late.

Yes, she is.

Nothing important.

3d

Why do they use the expressions?

C

1

Watch to JULIA: ... *doesn't need me.* **Answer the questions.**

1 What is Julia doing?

2 Where's Frederick?

3 How does this help Julia?

2

Watch again. Match the responses to the questions and suggestions.

1	Are there any places in there?	a	I can't afford that.
2	What about this?	b	I was late this morning, remember?
3	You could try an agency.	c	So Martha doesn't need me.
4	Ask Martha for some time off ...	d	No, there aren't.
5	Martha's got a teleconference ...	e	I haven't got time.

3

Watch again. Complete the advertisement.

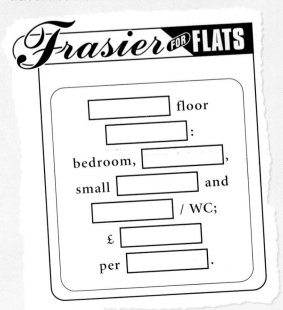

Frasier **FOR FLATS**

⬭ floor

⬭ :

bedroom, ⬭ , small ⬭ and ⬭ / WC;

£ ⬭

per ⬭ .

29

D

1

Watch to JULIA: *OK.* **Answer the questions.**

1   Does Julia find a place to live?

2   Who is Mr Jackson?

3   What do the people upstairs do?

4   Where does Julia go with Rebecca? Why?

5   Who else goes?

2a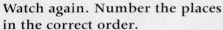

Watch again. Number the places in the correct order.

d

a

2b

What does Julia say about the places?

- too far away
- too small
- too expensive
- very strange
- too noisy
- just grotty
- too dark

2c

Which descriptions could you use for the places in the pictures?

3

Watch again. Complete Julia's conversation with Mr Jackson.

JULIA: *So, let _____ see. There's the _____ and the _____, and the _____ and the _____ are in the _____.*

MR JACKSON: *Yes, that's right. You _____ them with the people _____. They're very _____ people.*

JULIA: *And how _____ is it, Mr Jackson?*

MR JACKSON: *It's only £ _____ a _____.*

4a

Watch again. Who says each thing?

(_____): *So are you interested?*

(_____): *Any luck?*

(_____): *Never mind.*

4b

What do they mean?

b

c

E

1

Watch to REBECCA: *Sssh, everybody. It's Ellie.* What is Gary saying?

2

Watch again. Choose the correct endings.

1 The bathroom in Rebecca's flat is …

☐ next to Rebecca's bedroom.

☐ next to Ellie's room.

☐ upstairs.

2 Gary lives …

☐ next door.

☐ about a mile away.

☐ just round the corner.

3 His flat is …

☐ on the top floor.

☐ on the sixth floor.

☐ on the ground floor.

4 Rebecca offers everyone …

☐ tea.

☐ wine.

☐ coffee.

5 The first message on the answerphone … is from

☐ Ellie.

☐ Rebecca's sister.

☐ Tim.

6 Gary calls Tim …

☐ a romantic fool.

☐ very sweet.

☐ an old romantic.

3

Watch again. Tick the correct answers.

1 Which rooms does Rebecca mention?

☐ living room

☐ bedroom

☐ dining room

☐ bathroom

☐ kitchen

☐ toilet

☐ hall

2 What does she say about Gary's flat?

☐ It's a lovely place.

☐ It's very nice.

☐ It's got a great view.

☐ It's very big.

☐ It's very expensive.

3 What does Tim say in his message?

☐ Hi. It's me. Tim.

☐ Happy birthday to you.

☐ I love you, Ellie.

☐ See you later.

☐ Love you. Bye.

F

1

Watch to the end of Episode 4. Answer the questions.

1 Who says each thing?

[ ] : *I'm really sorry about this.*

[ ] : *Oh dear. Poor Tim.*

[ ] : *Well, it was very strange.*

[ ] : *Look on the bright side.*

[ ] : *Gary!*

[ ] : *Gary's right.*

[ ] : *That's great! Wonderful!*

[ ] : *Oh, Tim. I'm sorry.*

2 Why do they say them?

3 What does Tim say?

2

Watch again. Complete Ellie's message.

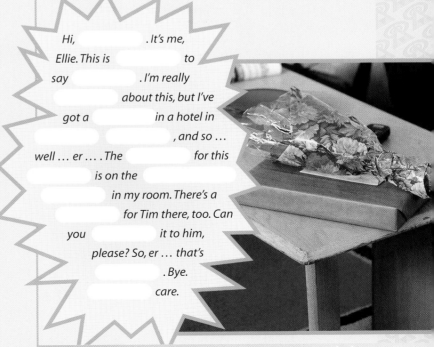

Hi, _____ . It's me, Ellie. This is _____ to say _____ . I'm really _____ about this, but I've got a _____ in a hotel in _____ , and so … well … er … . The _____ for this is on the _____ in my room. There's a _____ for Tim there, too. Can you _____ it to him, please? So, er … that's _____ . Bye. _____ care.

▲ Watch the whole of Episode 4 again. ◄◄

31

Exercises

1a

Go round the class. Talk to ten people and find out when their birthdays are.

Example

> When's your birthday?
>
> It's the second of May.

1b

Write down the birthdays.

Example

Pedro: 2 May

2

Work with a partner. Look at the information board. Ask where the places are.

Example

> Excuse me. Where can I find the gym?
>
> It's on the fifth floor.
>
> Thank you.

THE TOWER CONFERENCE CENTRE
Floor

10	The Oasis Restaurant
9	Managing Director's office
8	Library
7	Communications Centre
6	Meeting rooms
5	Gym and swimming pool
4	Shops, telephones, toilets
3	Conference Rooms C and D
2	Coffee shop and bar
1	Reception
Ground	Car park

3

Complete the conversations with *was*, *wasn't*, *were* or *weren't*.

1

MARTHA: You _____ late again this morning, Julia.

JULIA: But it _____ my fault. There _____ an accident at the station and there _____ any trains for five hours.

MARTHA: I know, but nobody else _____ late. And you _____ late on Monday and last Thursday, too.

JULIA: Yes, I'm sorry.

2

Gary: What _____ the houses like?

JULIA: Oh, they _____ terrible. One of them _____ a houseboat, so it _____ very small. And another one _____ really grotty.

GARY: _____ there any good places?

JULIA: Well, three of them were OK, but the first one _____ too far away and the second one _____ too expensive.

GARY: I see. What _____ the third one like?

JULIA: That _____ bad at all. There _____ a room and a kitchen. The bathroom and the toilet _____ in the hall.

GARY: How much _____ the rent?

JULIA: It _____ only £65 a week.

GARY: So what _____ the problem?

JULIA: It _____ too noisy. There _____ some people upstairs and they play rock music.

GARY: Oh dear.

4

Here are some of the things that Julia and the people at the houses said. Complete them with the correct form of *there is / are*.

1. How many rooms _____ ?
2. _____ two people upstairs.
3. _____ a bathroom?
4. _____ a toilet downstairs.
5. _____ a garden behind the house.
6. _____ some students in the next flat.

7. _____ two bedrooms?
8. How many chairs _____ in the kitchen?
9. _____ a television in the living room?
10. _____ a telephone?
11. _____ a bus stop at the end of the road.
12. How many flats _____ in the house?

32

5

Look at page 31.
Describe Rebecca's flat. Use
there's / are or *there isn't / aren't.*

Examples

There are two bedrooms.
There isn't a balcony.
There's a table in the living
  room.

6a

Work with a partner. Student A
cover picture B. Student B cover
picture A. Ask questions about
your partner's place. Use

Is there a ... ?

How many ... are there?

Where is the ... ?

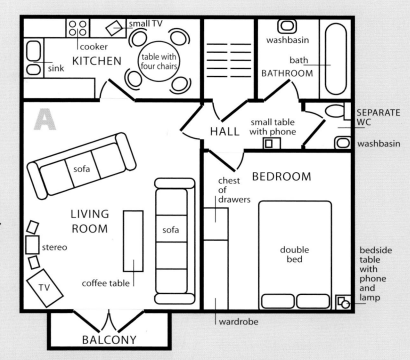

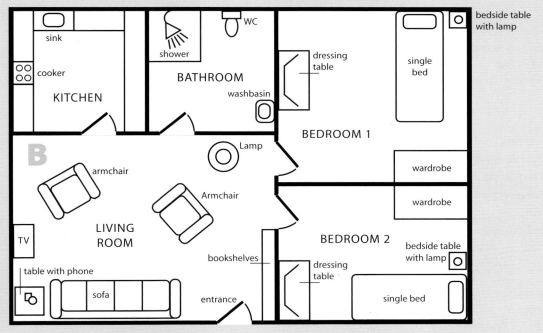

6b

One of the flats above is your new flat.
Write ten sentences to describe it.

Role play

**Work in pairs. Write and act a play
to fit this scenario.**

Student A is looking for a place to live.

Student B takes the role of three people who
own or share the flats.

Student A goes to see three flats. He / she
asks Student B about the flats. There are
problems with the first two. Student A
makes his / her excuses and leaves.
The third flat is fine. Student A asks about
it and agrees to take it.

Language in use

1 Useful expressions

Complete the dialogues with the expressions.

1

Look on the bright side   Any luck
Never mind   No, I suppose not

A: I was in a race yesterday.
B: _____ ?
A: No. I was last.
B: _____ . You can't win them all.
A: _____ .
B: Yes _____ .
You can only get better.

2

remember   Really
I'm really sorry about this
it wasn't my fault
can I take some time off

A: _____ , but _____ this morning?
B: You have to finish the Newcastle report , _____ ?
A: I can do that this afternoon.
B: The last report was late.
A: Yes, but _____ . The computers were down.
B: OK. You can take two hours off.
A: _____ ? Oh, thank you.

3

Are you interested   I can't afford that
How much is it   a week
that's it   if you want it

A: Well, _____ .
B: So there's the room and I share the kitchen and the bathroom?
A: Yes, that's right. _____ ?
B: Yes, definitely.
A: Well, the room is yours, _____ .
B: _____ ?
A: Its £100 _____ .
B: Oh dear, _____ .

2 Responses

Match the expressions in the two columns to make dialogues. Some can go with more than one.

		a	I know. I'm sorry.
1	Come to my place for a drink.	b	OK. Thanks.
2	There was an accident here yesterday.	c	Never mind.
3	I was up at five o'clock this morning.	d	Yes, that's right.
4	Is our meeting at ten o'clock?	e	Yes, you look tired.
5	Tea, everyone?	f	Its the tenth of July.
6	Back in a minute.	g	Yes, please.
7	I can't make it for lunch today.	h	OK.
8	You're late.	i	I'm sorry. I don't know.
9	What's the date today?	j	Oh dear!
		k	Really?
		l	Let me see.

Culture note: living away from home

It is unusual in Britain for young adults to live with their parents. Most young people move out to a place of their own as soon as they can afford it.

Young people often share a flat with one or two other people. Each person normally has their own bedroom and they share the other rooms like the kitchen, living room and bathroom. This is cheaper and provides some company.

Instead of a flat, a lot of young people live in a bedsit. This is a room that serves as both a bedroom and a living room. The bedsit may have its own kitchen and / or bathroom, but very often you have to share these with people in other bedsits in the house. A bedsit is usually a lot cheaper than a flat.

34

Grammar summary

The Past simple tense of *to be*

Positive statements

I He She It	was	here at home late	on Monday. last night. yesterday.
We You They	were		

Negative statements

I He She It	wasn't (was not)	here at home late	on Monday. last night. yesterday.
You We They	weren't (were not)		

Questions

Was	I he she it	here at home late	on Monday? last night? yesterday?
Were	you we they		

Short answers

Yes,	I was. you were.	No,	I wasn't. you weren't.

there is / there are

We use *there is* for singular countable nouns and uncountable nouns.

We use *there are* for plural countable nouns.

Present simple	There is …	There are …
Past simple	There was …	There were …
Negative	There isn't … There wasn't …	There aren't … There weren't
Question	Is there …? Was there …?	Are there …? Were there …?

There's a letter here for Tim.

There was an accident at the station.

Are there any places in there?

Ordinals

1st	first	11th	eleventh
2nd	second	12th	twelfth
3rd	third	13th	thirteenth
4th	fourth	14th	fourteenth
5th	fifth	15th	fifteenth
6th	sixth	20th	twentieth
7th	seventh	21st	twenty-first
8th	eighth	30th	thirtieth
9th	ninth	32nd	thirty-second
10th	tenth	100th	hundredth

My room's on the **sixth** floor.

Her birthday is on the **thirty-first** of May.

She was **third** in the exam.

Dates

When we write dates we usually use the short form.

It was on December 6.

The date is 12 July.

We can say dates in two different ways. We put in *the* and *of*.

December 6

*The sixth **of** December.* or *December **the** sixth.*

12 July

*The twelfth **of** July.* or *July **the** twelfth.*

EPISODE 5

Life's too short

A

1

Watch to **REBECCA:** *Have a nice day.*
Number the pictures in the correct
order.

a

f

b

2

Answer the questions.

1 Who is late? Why?

2 Who is in a bad mood? Why?

3 Who is happy? Why?

3a

Watch again. Match the halves of
the sentences.

: 1 I'm sorry	**a**	on, Sean.
: 2 Not	**b**	he's in a bad mood.
: 3 We need to	**c**	go in five minutes.
: 4 What's the	**d**	what to do.
: 5 It's	**e**	Ellie.
: 6 She's	**f**	all bad news ...
: 7 We didn't know	**g**	a nice day.
: 8 No wonder	**h**	now, Sean.
: 9 But it's not	**i**	matter with him today?
: 10 Come	**j**	all day.
: 11 We haven't got	**k**	I'm late, Tim.
: 12 Have	**l**	gone.

c

d

e

3b

Who says each thing?

36

4

Watch again. Rebecca hesitates after she says *She left yesterday*. **Why?**

5

Read what Rebecca says. Some of it is wrong. Watch again and correct it.

REBECCA: *You see, it* ~~it~~ *yesterday was Ellie's birthday. Tim, Gary, Julia and I went back to my flat for a birthday meal for Ellie. She wasn't there, but there was a message from her on the answerphone. She said that she had a job in New York and well ... that's it.*

SEAN: *What did Tim do?*

REBECCA: *He just left the flat. He didn't say anything. It was all very sad and, well, difficult. We didn't know what to say.*

1a

Look at the picture and answer the questions.

1 What is happening?

2 Who is helping?

1b

Watch to JULIA: *So who can we invite?* **Check your ideas.**

2

Watch again. Tick the correct endings.

1 Rebecca offers Mr Drake ...

☐ a cup of coffee. ☐ a glass of beer.

☐ a cup of tea.

2 The flat is in ...

☐ Wellington Gardens. ☐ Western Avenue.

☐ Garden Road.

3 Rebecca and Julia decide to ...

☐ have a party. ☐ go to meet the neighbours.

☐ invite the neighbours for a drink.

4 Rebecca calls it ...

☐ a *Hello Julia* event.

☐ a sort of *Welcome to Julia* thing.

☐ something to say *Welcome Julia*.

5 They decide to do it ...

☐ at the weekend. ☐ next Friday.

☐ on Saturday evening.

6 Frederick is in ...

☐ South America. ☐ Southampton.

☐ South Africa.

7 He's away ...

☐ for two weeks.

☐ for the rest of the week.

☐ until next week.

3a

Watch again. Complete the expressions.

1 ⬭ : *That's* ⬭ .

2 ⬭ : *I'd better* ⬭ .

3 ⬭ : *Don't mention* ⬭ .

4 ⬭ : *Welcome* ⬭ .

5 ⬭ : *I still can't* ⬭ .

6 ⬭ : *Why don't we* ⬭ ?

7 ⬭ : *Everyone? Even* ⬭ ?

8 ⬭ : *Don't* ⬭ .

3b

Who says each thing?

37

C

1

Watch to TIM: *... I think we can take a look at that now.* **Number the pictures in the correct order.**

2

Watch again. Write the expressions in the speech bubbles.

> *We've got that programme to finish.*
> *We can't come.*
> *I think we can take a look at that now.*
> *Can't we do it another time?*
> *Tim, here.*
> *It's an invitation to our party.*
> *It's party time!*
> *No!*
> *No, it isn't.*
> *What's this?*

3a

What do you think of Tim's behaviour?

3b

What would you do if you were Sean or Julia?

D

1

Watch to TIM: *Why did you give up your job ... ?* **Answer the questions.**

1 What are Tim and Sean doing?

2 Who is the man on the TV screens?

2

Watch again. Complete Tim's commentary.

> *Last year _____ gave up his job in a _____ and decided to _____ to the _____ .*

3

What questions do you think Tim will ask the man?

E

1

Did Richard succeed? Watch to
RICHARD: ... *ten metres deep.* and find out.

2

Watch again. Tick the correct answers.

1 When did he leave England?

☐ August   ☐ October

☐ September

2 Where did he go first?

☐ Argentina   ☐ Chile

☐ Brazil

3 Why did he have to wait for a few weeks?

☐ Someone stole his money.

☐ He was ill.

☐ The weather was bad.

4 When did he set off?

☐ August   ☐ October

☐ September

5 Did he go ...

☐ with two friends?

☐ on his own?

☐ with his brother?

6 How far did he walk before his accident?

☐ 200 kilometres

☐ 300 kilometres

☐ 350 kilometres

7 What happened to him?

☐ He lost his map.

☐ There was an avalanche.

☐ He fell into a crevasse.

3a

Tick the reasons he gives for making
the journey.

1 His wife left him.   ☐

2 He didn't like his job.   ☐

3 He had a lot of problems at home.   ☐

4 He wanted to do something different.   ☐

5 He wanted to get away from it all.   ☐

6 He wanted to write a book.   ☐

7 He wanted to find himself.   ☐

3b

Watch again. Check your answers.

3c

What do you think of his reasons?

F

1a

What do you think happened to
Richard? How did he get back to
England?

1b

Watch to **SEAN:** *Yes, that's fine.* Check your
ideas.

2

Watch again. Are these statements true
(T) or false (F)?

1 Richard broke his leg. ☐

2 He climbed out of the hole. ☐

3 He lost his sledge. ☐

4 He didn't have any food. ☐

5 He called for help on his radio. ☐

6 He was in the hole for six days. ☐

7 People couldn't rescue him because there was a storm. ☐

8 The rescuers had some dogs with them. ☐

9 Richard thought about his family and friends when he was in the crevasse. ☐

10 Tim wants to watch the last part again. ☐

3a

Watch again. Complete what Richard
says.

*I thought about my _____ back in
_____. And the _____ thing
was that all my _____ at home and at
_____ weren't _____ any more.
I just _____ to be with my _____
and _____ again. Life's very
_____, you know. You have to
_____ it while you _____.*

3b

Do you agree with Richard? How do his
ideas apply to Tim?

G

1

Look at the picture.
Watch to the end and
answer the questions.

1 How does Tim react to Sean's offer?

2 Why?

3 Do Tim and Sean have a cup of coffee?

Would you like a cup of coffee?

39

▲ Watch the whole of Episode 5 again. ◄◄

Exercises

1

Write a summary of this episode. Use these cues.

Example

1   Sean / be / late for work
   Sean was late for work.
2   Tim / shout / at him
3   Tim / be / in a bad mood about Ellie
4   Rebecca / tell / Sean about Ellie
5   Julia / move / into the flat
6   Her father / help / her
7   Rebecca and Julia / decide / to have a party

8   Julia /give / invitations to Sean and Tim
9   Tim / not want / to go
10   Sean and Julia/ not know / what to do
11   Tim / not go / to the party
12   He / go / to finish a programme with Sean
13   The programme / make / Tim think about his own life
14   Tim and Sean / go / to the party

2

Complete Richard Bennett's story. Use the verbs in brackets in the Past simple tense.

Until last year Richard Bennett _____ (be) just another office worker. Every day he _____ (travel) to London by train and _____ (work) from nine till five in a bank. But he _____ (not like) his job and he also _____ (have) a lot of problems with his family. Richard _____ (want) to get away from it all. So he _____ (decide) to walk to the South Pole.

Last August he _____ (give up) his job at the bank and _____ (fly) to Buenos Aires. From there he _____ (take) a boat to the Antarctic. He _____ (arrive) there at the end of August, but he _____ (not leave) the base until the end of September because the weather _____ (not be) very good.

Finally the weather _____ (change) and he _____ (set off) to the South Pole, but he _____ (not reach) it. He _____ (walk) for about three hundred kilometres and then he _____ (fall) into a crevasse and he _____ (break) his arm. The crevasse _____ (be) ten metres deep, so he _____ (can't) climb out. Luckily his sledge _____ (fall) into the crevasse, too, so he _____ (have) food and a radio. He _____ (call) for help, but a bad storm _____ (start). So the rescuers _____ (can't) look for him. Richard _____ (stay) in the crevasse for five days. He _____ (think) it was the end for him, but suddenly he _____ (hear) voices and dogs. He _____ (shout) and the rescuers _____ (find) him.

3

Tim is interviewing someone else. Complete Tim's questions. Use these verbs.

feel	leave	reach	go	think (2)	learn
decide	sail	reach	fall	do	have	be (2)

Example

Tim: *Rita Lee is sixty years old, but last year she decided to sail around the world. When* **did you learn** *to sail a boat, Rita?*

Rita: *I learnt to sail when I was a child. My father loved boats.*

Tim: *Why _____ to sail around the world?*

Rita: *I just wanted to do something different.*

Tim: *_____ your husband _____ with you?*

Rita: *No, he didn't. I went on my own.*

Tim: *What _____ he _____ of the idea?*

Rita: *He thought I was mad, but he helped me a lot.*

Tim: *When _____ England?*

Rita: *I left at the end of May.*

Tim: *And where _____ to first?*

Rita: *I sailed to Brazil and then round South America and on to Australia.*

Tim: *_____ Australia?*

Rita: *No, I didn't. There was a bad storm and my boat turned over.*

Tim: *_____ out of the boat?*

Rita: *Yes, I did, but I swam under the boat and stayed there. It was upside down, but there was air inside it. So it wasn't too bad.*

Tim: *_____ a radio?*

Rita: *Yes, fortunately, I had a radio and some water.*

Tim: *_____ there any food in the boat?*

Rita: *No, there wasn't, so I was very hungry.*

Tim: *How long _____ inside the boat?*

Rita: *I was there for three days and then suddenly I heard voices.*

Tim: *What _____ when you heard the voices?*

Rita: *I swam out and I saw a small boat and a big ship there.*

Tim: *How _____ ?*

Rita: *I felt wonderful. It was great.*

Tim: *What _____ about while you were in the boat?*

Rita: *I thought about my life and my family, but I didn't worry about things. I believe that when it's your time to go, you have to go. So it's silly to worry.*

Tim: *Thank you very much, Rita.*

4

Correct these statements about Rita's adventure.

Example

1 She wanted to get away from it all.

   She didn't want to get away from it all. She just wanted to do something different.

2 Her husband went with her.

3 She sailed to Florida first.

4 Her boat sank.

5 She stayed on top of the boat.

6 She had some food.

7 She was in the boat for five days.

8 When she heard voices she shouted.

Work in pairs. Write and act a play to fit this scenario.

Last year Student A did something unusual. It went wrong, but it taught him / her an important lesson about life. Student B interviews Student A about his / her experience.

Language in use

1a Useful expressions

Match the expressions to their meanings.

1	Not now.*	a	That's all right.
2	He didn't say a word.	b	Goodbye.
3	Come on. I haven't got all day.*	c	I want to leave all my problems.
4	Have a nice day.	d	He said nothing.
5	That's the lot.	e	I have to go.
6	I'd better be off.	f	I haven't got time now.
7	Don't mention it.	g	Hurry up.
8	Don't worry.	h	I can express it like this.
9	I want to get away from it all.	i	There isn't any more.
10	… if you like.	j	It's not a problem.

*Note: these expressions show impatience and are not very polite.

1b

How do you say these things in your language?

2 Responses

Give appropriate responses to the statements. Use the table.

Example

1 Tim's girlfriend left him.

No wonder he's annoyed.

No wonder	he she	's annoyed. 's in a bad mood. 's late. 's annoyed. isn't here today. looks tired. looks pleased.

2 Julia's got a flat.

3 Gary was up at three o'clock this morning.

4 Rebecca's ill.

5 Martha lost her bag yesterday.

6 Sean had to go to the police station.

3 Dialogues

Make dialogues. Use the tables.

Example

A: Can we meet for lunch today?

B: Im sorry. Ive got some shopping to do.

Can	you I we	come to our party? work late tonight? have a word? meet for lunch? talk about the conference? make a meeting at two? play tennis on Saturday?

I'm sorry. Not now.*	I've got	a party a conference some letters a report some people a meeting a programme some work some shopping	to	go to. write. meet. finish. do.

4 Decisions

What would you say in these situations? Use *I'd better* … .

Example

1 Someone offers you a drink, but you haven't got time.

No thanks. I'd better be off.

2 You have to get up at 7 o'clock. It's now 7.05.

3 You have to go to meet some people at the station at 9.30. It's now 9.15.

4 There isn't any food in the fridge.

5 It's late and you are very tired.

6 There isn't much petrol in your car.

7 It's your boyfriend's / girlfriend's birthday tomorrow.

Culture note: parties

It is traditional to have a party when someone moves into a new house. It is called a *housewarming party*.

People usually take a bottle of wine to a party. You can also take a bunch of flowers or a box of chocolates, but normally only if the person giving the party is a woman.

Grammar summary

The Past simple tense – regular verbs

We use the Past simple tense to talk about completed actions or states in the past.

To make the regular form of the Past simple tense we add –ed or –d.

Positive statements

I You He She It We They	walked sailed	to the Antarctic. to the North Pole. around the world.

The Past simple tense – spelling

We add –ed to verbs ending in a consonant.

wait happen	waited happened

We add –d to verbs ending in e.

love change	loved changed

We take away the y and add –ied to verbs ending in consonant + y.

worry try	worried tried

We add an extra consonant to verbs ending in consonant + vowel + consonant.

travel stop	travelled stopped

The Past simple tense – pronunciation

After voiced sounds we pronounce the final d as /d/.

/d/ travelled called appeared

After unvoiced sounds we pronounce the final d as /t/.

/t/ helped worked walked

When a verb ends in t or d we pronounce the final syllable /ɪd/.

/ɪd/ decided shouted wanted

The Past simple tense – irregular verbs

A lot of common verbs have an irregular past form.

go	went	learn	learnt
have	had	leave	left
give	gave	make	made
think	thought	take	took
swim	swam	break	broke
hear	heard	sink	sank
fall	fell	see	saw
teach	taught	feel	felt

Negative statements

I You He She It We You They	didn't (did not)	reach Australia. like the job. go abroad. fall out of the boat.

Questions

Did	I you he she it we they	reach Australia? like the job? go abroad? fall out of the boat?

In questions and negatives we use the stem form of the verb, not the Past tense form.

She didn't **reach** Australia.

Short answers

Yes,	I did. he did. she did.	No,	I didn't. he didn't. she didn't.

Questions, negative statements and short answers are the same for both regular and irregular verbs.

Wh – questions

When did you give up your job?

What did they think of the programme?

How long did you stay inside the boat?

Time expressions

Time expressions are often used with the Past simple tense.

last year	yesterday	in May
last month	this morning	in 1963
last night	on Monday	a year ago

Time expressions usually come at the beginning or end of the sentence.

Last year she travelled to New York.

or

She travelled to New York last year.

43

EPISODE 6

Sharp-dressed man

While you watch

A

1

Watch to JULIA: *Let's see what he's buying.* **Answer the questions.**

1 Where are Julia and Rebecca going?
2 Who comes in while they are there?
3 Why is he / she there?
4 Where does he / she go?
5 What do Julia and Rebecca do when they see him / her?

2a

Complete what Julia says. Who is she quoting?

> Oh yes. What did he say? The _____ of _____ and Style voted me the _____ -dressed _____ on _____.

2b

Watch again. Check your answers.

3a

What is Julia looking at? Tick the correct things.

£25.80

£26.40

£28.50

£30.95

£42.60

3b

Match the things to the correct price tags.

3c

Watch again. Check your answers.

B

1

Watch to **GARY:** *Hi, Tim.* Answer the questions.

1 What is Gary looking for?

2 What does he ask the assistant?

2a

Watch again. Complete what Gary says.

Only the _____ is _____ _____ for the _____ – _____ .

2b

How do Julia and Rebecca react?

3a

Look at these sentences. Choose the correct form of the verb. Delete the incorrect ones.

1 (_____): Hi, Gary. What
 do you do?
 are you doing?

2 (_____): I
 look
 'm looking for a shirt and tie.

3 (_____): Oh
 do you know
 are you knowing about that?

4 (_____): Everybody
 knows.
 is knowing.

5 (_____): You
 mention
 're mentioning it at least ten times a day.

6 (_____): How many shirts
 do you take?
 are you taking?

3b

Who says each thing?

3c

Watch again. Check your answers.

C

1

Watch until Gary goes to the dressing room. Are these statements true (T) or false (F)?

1 Gary is wearing his new suit.

2 He tries to hide the bags from Tim.

3 The suit is by Gucci.

4 Tim doesn't know about Gary's interview.

5 The interview is after the news.

GIORGIO ARMANI

2a

Watch again. Who says each thing? How do they say them? Why?

1 (_____): Hi, Tim.

2 (_____): OK, Gary. What's in the bags?

3 (_____): Oh, these?

4 (_____): ... the best-dressed newsreader.

5 (_____): Yes, we know.

2b

At the end Tim, Julia and Rebecca all look at each other. What do you think they're going to do?

3

Watch again. Complete the expressions.

TIM: _____ , eh? Bet that cost a _____ .

GARY: Well, if it's _____ , the _____ doesn't matter.

TIM: Did you _____ that?

JULIA: Yes, he's even _____ than usual.

TIM: _____ should do _____ about him. When is this interview _____ ?

REBECCA: _____ after the six o'clock news.

45

D

1a

Look at the pictures. What is happening in each one?

1b

Number the pictures.

1c

Watch to the end of Episode 6. Check your answers.

a

b

c

d

e

f

g

h

j

APEX TV NEWS

i

k

2

Watch again. Answer the questions.

1 Why does Tim go into the dressing room twice?

2 Why doesn't Gary see him?

3 What does Gary do with Sean's trousers?

46

E

 1

Rewind the tape to MARTHA: *Gary. Your visitors.* Watch to JULIA: *What's happening?*

What's this woman's name?

Charlie Morgan

Charlotte Mortimer

Sharon Morris

 2

Watch again. Answer the questions.

1 What does the reporter want to do first?

2 Where does Gary want to sit?

3 Why does he say he wants to sit there?

4 What does the reporter think the readers want to see?

 3

Watch again. Match the halves of the sentences.

1	... may I	a	take some photographs first?
2	... can we	b	more comfortable here.
3	We always see	c	be shy.
4	Well, I feel	d	call you Gary?
5	... I'd really prefer	e	is better.
6	Come on now, Gary. Don't	f	you at your desk.
7	... perhaps at the desk	g	to be at my desk.

 4

Watch again. Underline the word that the reporter stresses. What does she imply?

What are you wearing?

F

 1

Watch to GARY: *Photograph? Are these statements true (T) or false (F)?*

1 Rebecca, Tim and Julia are in the control room.

2 They're watching Gary's interview.

3 Gary is enjoying the interview.

4 Julia says they should give Gary his trousers back.

5 Tim tells Gary that he took the trousers.

6 Gary goes to the dressing room to change his trousers.

7 He throws the old trousers away.

8 Gary sits on his desk for the photographs.

 2

Watch again. Choose the correct form of the verb. Delete the incorrect one.

1 What   happens? / 's happening?

2 The reporter   interviews / 's interviewing   Gary.

3 And Gary   always enjoys / is always enjoying   interviews.

4 Well, he   doesn't enjoy / isn't enjoying   this one.

5 I   think / 'm thinking   we should give his trousers back now.

G

 1

Watch to the end. Where are Gary, Julia, Tim and Rebecca? Where is Sean?

2a

Watch again. Complete the expressions.

1 (   ): *Come   , Gary. Cheer   . The magazine got   of you in your new   in the   .*

2 (   ): *But you looked so   in those   old trousers.*

3 (   ):   *did you get   anyway?*

4 (   ):   *were Sean's. Oh, Sean!*

2b

Who says each thing?

▲ Watch the whole of Episode 6 again. ◄◄

47

Exercises

1a

Look at the photographs. What are the people wearing?

1b

Are they carrying anything?

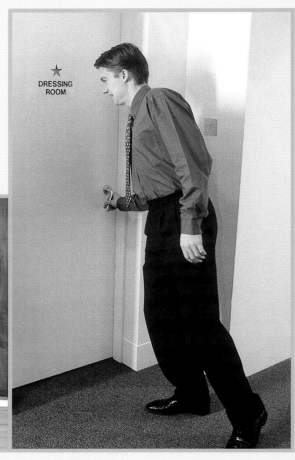

48

2a

Complete what Julia says. What do you notice about *trousers*?

The skirt ⬜⬜⬜ £28.50. The trousers ⬜⬜⬜ a bit more expensive.

2b

Complete the dialogues. Use these words.

| it's | is | this | it |

A: Do you like ⬜⬜ shirt?

B: Yes. ⬜⬜ fine. How much ⬜⬜ ?

A: ⬜⬜ £23.

B: Why don't you try ⬜⬜ on?

Later

A: How is ⬜⬜ ?

B: ⬜⬜ too big, but they haven't got ⬜⬜ in a smaller size.

A: Oh well, never mind.

2c

Change *shirt* to *shorts* and write the dialogue again.

2d

Work with a partner. Read your dialogues.

3a

Compare Julia and Rebecca. Use these words.

long   short   dark   fair   relaxed   attractive   organized

Example

Julia has got longer hair than Rebecca.

3b

Compare Tim and Gary. Write six sentences.

4a

What do you think of the characters in *Lifetime*?

Use the superlatives of these words and write down your ideas.

nice   interesting   good   funny   good-looking
annoying   attractive   serious   well-dressed

Example

I think Rebecca is the nicest person.

4b

Compare your opinions with a partner.

5

Complete the texts. Put the verbs in brackets into the Present simple tense or the Present continuous.

Work in a group of three. Write and act a play to fit this scenario.

Student A and Student B are friends. They go into a clothes shop. Student C is the shop assistant.

Student A tries on lots of different clothes, but doesnt like anything. He / she asks for something bigger, smaller, darker, lighter, etc. In the end Student A decides not to buy anything. The assistant by now is very annoyed.

49

1

This is Gary. In this photograph he _____ (read) the news. He _____ (read) the news every day. Here he _____ (read) the evening news, but sometimes he _____ (read) the breakfast news.

2

Sean is a cameraman. He always _____ (work) with Tim. They often _____ (do) reports on people. In this picture Tim _____ (try) to interview a man called Carl Stalker. Sean _____ (film) them. Stalker _____ (run) a company called *Wonderful Windows*. He _____ (take) his customers' money, but he _____ (not deliver) the windows.

3

In this photograph Julia _____ (go) to work. She _____ (say) goodbye to her parents. Her father, Colin, _____ (have) his breakfast. He _____ (not pay) any attention to Julia, because he _____ (read) his newspaper. Julia _____ (not live) with her parents any more. She _____ (live) with Rebecca. They _____ (share) a flat in town. Julia _____ (go) to see her parents every couple of weeks and she often _____ (talk) to them on the phone.

Language in use

1a Modifiers

Complete the table with these words.

a   bit   much

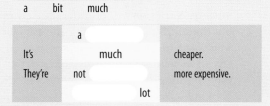

	a		
It's		much	cheaper.
They're	not		more expensive.
		lot	

1b

Compare these things. Use the table.

Example

The trousers are a bit cheaper than the jacket.

2a Expressing surprise

Sentence stress changes the meaning of the question. This is a normal question:

■   ■

What are you wearing?

This expresses surprise:

■   ■

What are you wearing?

2b

Say these with normal stress and again with surprised stress.

1   *Where is she going?*

2   *What are they doing?*

3   *What is he watching?*

4   *What are you eating?*

5   *What is she looking at?*

6   *What are you listening to?*

3 Useful expressions

Complete the dialogues with the expressions.

it doesn't go with that shirt
Let's see what's happening
do something about
Cheer up
there you are
What do you think
I bet
Sorry to interrupt
Look

1

A: *Oh,* _____ . *Why are you late?*

2

A: _____ , *but the Managing Director's on the phone.*

3

A: *You look a bit sad.* _____ .

4

A: *I like this tie.* _____ ?

B: *It's all right, but* _____ .

5

A: _____ . *They're making a film over there.*

B: *Come on.* _____ .

6

A: *Tim decided to* _____ *Gary, so he took his trousers.*

B: _____ *Gary was annoyed.*

4a Dialogues

Look at the table. Add two more expressions.

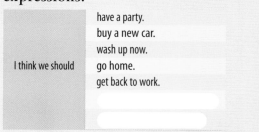

	have a party.
I think we should	buy a new car.
	wash up now.
	go home.
	get back to work.

4b

Make dialogues. Use the table and the expressions below.

Oh, all right.

I suppose you're right.

That's a good idea.

50

Grammar summary

The Present continuous tense

We use the Present continuous tense to talk about

- actions taking place at the time of speaking

He's going into the men's department.

The reporter's interviewing Gary.

- temporary activities around the time of speaking

I'm learning English.

He's staying in London.

We make the Present continuous tense using the present of *to be* + … *ing*.

Positive statements

I He	'm (am)	
She It	's (is)	looking for a shirt. buying a new car. interviewing Gary.
We You They	're (are)	

Negative statements

I	'm not (am not)	
He She It	isn't (is not)	wearing a tie. coming to the meeting. working today.
We You They	aren't (are not)	

Questions

Am	I	
Is	he she it	buying some clothes? enjoying the party? watching the news?
Are	you they	

Short answers

Yes,	I am. he is. she is.		No,	I'm not. he isn't. she isn't.

Comparatives and superlatives

To make comparatives we add *-er* to the adjective.

To make superlatives we add *-est*

adjective	comparative	superlative
small	smaller	the smallest
long	longer	the longest

For adjectives ending in *-e* we add *-r* or *-st*.

nice	nicer	the nicest

For adjectives with a short vowel + consonant we double the consonant.

big	bigger	the biggest

For adjectives ending in *-y* we take away *-y* and add *-ier* or *-iest*.

lazy	lazier	the laziest

For most adjectives with two or more syllables we put *more* or *most* in front of the adjective.

important	more important	the most important
expensive	more expensive	the most expensive

Some comparatives and superlatives are irregular.

good	better	the best
bad	worse	the worst
far	further	the furthest

a bit / much / a lot / + comparative

We use *a bit, much, a lot* to say if the difference between two items is small or big.

If there is a small difference.

£29.99	£28.99

*These trousers are **a bit** more expensive than those.*

If there is a big difference.

£35.00	£19.00

*This tie is **a lot** more expensive than that one.*
or
*This tie is **much** more expensive than that one.*

Clothes

Some clothes are always plural.

trousers, tights, shorts, jeans

We use plural articles and verbs with these words.

I like these trousers.

How much are they?

To give quantities of plural words we use *pair(s) of*.

a pair of two pairs of	jeans trousers shorts socks shoes

EPISODE 7
The end or the beginning?

1a

Look at the picture. What do you think is happening?

1b

Watch to JULIA: … *doctor.* Answer the questions.

1   Where are they getting ready to go to?
2   Where do they actually go? Why?

2a

Are these statements true (T) or false (F)?

1   Tim's going to interview the headteacher.

2   She's won the lottery twice.

3   Sean has won the lottery.

4   Tim says he's got stomach-ache.

5   Julia thinks he should be in hospital.

6   Tim has often missed work because he's been ill.

7   Julia has done several interviews before.

8   Julia takes Tim to the doctor.

9   They go in Sean's car.

2b

Watch again. Check your answers.

3a

Read the dialogue, some parts of it are missing. Watch again. Put a mark (/) where something is missing.

JULIA: /Tim Are you all right?

TIM: Yes./I'm fine. I've just got stomach-ache.

JULIA: You can't work. You should be at home.

TIM: I've never missed work in my life and I'm not going to start. Anyway, who's going to do the interview if I'm not?

JULIA: Me.

TIM: Have you ever done an interview?

JULIA: No, I haven't, but I've watched you, and Sean's here. He's filmed interviews.

TIM: No, I can … Ow ah!

JULIA: Give me your keys. I'm going to take you to the doctor.

3b

Write in the missing parts.

3c

Watch again. Check your answers.

4

What do you think is going to happen to Tim?

52

B

1

Watch to GARY: … *twenty years ago.*
Answer the questions.

1   Where is Tim?

2   Who comes to see him?

3   What does each person bring?

4   Where does each person sit?

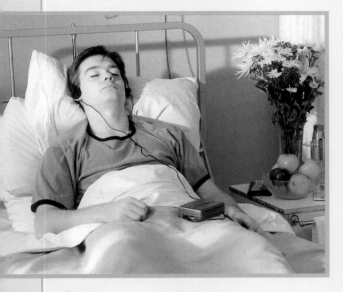

2a

Tick the correct endings.

1   Tim had …

☐ gastro-enteritis.

☐ tonsillitis.

☐ appendicitis.

2   He had his operation …

☐ this morning.

☐ yesterday afternoon.

☐ two hours ago.

3   Julia came to see him before, but …

☐ he was asleep.

☐ he couldn't have any visitors.

☐ he was still in the operating theatre.

4   Julia came …

☐ on her own.

☐ with Rebecca.

☐ with Martha and Gary.

5   Tim has …

☐ never been in hospital before.

☐ been in hospital once before.

☐ been in hospital twice before.

6   He's going to be in hospital until …

☐ tomorrow.

☐ Friday.

☐ next week.

7   Gary had appendicitis …

☐ at university.

☐ at school.

☐ on holiday.

8   He describes it as very …

☐ annoying.

☐ dangerous.

☐ painful.

2b

Watch again. Check your answers.

3

Watch again. Discuss the questions.

1   Who talks mostly about …

… work?

… himself / herself?

… Tim?

2   Complete the speech bubble.

> _____ had appendicitis, you know. Have you, _____ ?

Who says it? What's the answer?

3   What do Tim's visitors do while they are talking to him?

4   What do the characters' words and actions tell us about their personalities?

4

Why do you think Julia says this?

> I was with Rebecca.

53

C

1

Watch to TIM: … *Er, Julia.* **Answer the questions.**

1 What did the doctor say to Tim?

2 Why is Tim pleased?

2a

What do you think Tim is going to say to Julia?

2b

Watch to TIM: *Hi, Pete … .* **Check your ideas.**

2c

What is Julia's response?

3

Watch again. Number the dialogue in the correct order.

	I'm going to be in town anyway. So can we meet at the restaurant at say half past seven?
	Is this evening any good for you?
	Shall we try that new Italian place near the museum?
	Great. Shall I call for you about eight?
	OK.
	Mmm. That would be nice. When?
	… would you like to go out for a meal sometime?
	Yes, I'd love to.
	Yes, it's fine.

4a

Watch again. Complete what Tim says with these expressions.

_____, Julia … I, _____, wanted to say thank you for all your help when, _____ … and _____, _____ would you like to go out for a meal sometime, _____ to, _____, say thank you …

just	um
er	well
you know	

4b

What do the expressions show?

5

Watch again without the sound. Watch Tim's and Julia's expressions. What do they show about their feelings?

54

D

1

Watch to JULIA: *I can do it.* **Complete the sentences with the correct names.**

1 (_____) thinks the food is good.

2 (_____) loves Italian food.

3 (_____) lived in Italy.

4 (_____) worked in a travel company.

5 (_____) likes travelling.

6 (_____) has travelled around Asia and South America.

7 (_____) hasn't lived in another country.

8 (_____) has got sauce on his / her cheek.

9 (_____) is meeting some friends at the restaurant.

10 (_____) takes Tim's drink.

2

Watch again. Answer the questions.

1 What does Julia do when Tim tells her about the sauce?

2 What does Julia do when Gary tells her about the sauce?

3 What does she say to each one?

4 What do the different reactions show?

1a

Look at the pictures. What do you think happens?

1b

Watch to the end of Episode 7. Check your ideas.

2 📞

Watch again. Are these statements true (T) or false (F)?

1 Julia offers Tim a cup of coffee.

2 Tim has to be at work early tomorrow.

3 Tim says *Goodnight.* to Julia.

4 Julia can't find her keys.

5 Rebecca isn't in.

6 Rebecca is just going to see her sister.

7 Julia is locked out.

3a

Complete the speech bubbles with Tim's and Julia's last words.

3b

Julia isn't really locked out. So what do Tim and Julia mean?

1 Julia doesn't want to be in the flat while Rebecca is talking to her sister.

2 Tim and Julia want to spend a bit more time together, before Julia goes in.

3 Rebecca doesn't want Julia to come in while she is on the phone.

4 Rebecca is annoyed because Julia has lost her key.

4a

Some of the words and expressions in these sentences are not what the people actually say. Correct them.

1 *That was a really good dinner. I liked it.*

2 *I did, too, until Gary arrived.*

3 *Well, I've got an early job tomorrow.*

4 *Goodnight. See you in the morning.*

5 *I can't find my keys. I think I've left them at the restaurant.*

6 *Isn't Rebecca at home?*

7 *I'm not sure. Probably not.*

8 *I'm just phoning my sister. So I'll see you later.*

4b

Watch again. Check your answers.

5

Look at the title of Episode 7 and watch the last scene again. Answer the questions

1 What does the title mean?

2 Which is it – the beginning or the end?

3 What's going to happen next?

55

 Watch the whole of Episode 7 again. ◀◀

Exercises

1

What can you remember? What are the people going to do? Work with a partner. Ask and answer.

Example

What is Julia going to do here?

She's going to start work at Apex TV. She's going to catch the train.

2

Complete the sentences. Use these phrasal verbs in the Past simple tense.

travel around	go back
try on	call for
look after	go out for
take out	ask out

1 Tim _____ Julia _____ . They _____ a meal at an Italian restaurant.

2 Gary _____ several shirts and ties in the shop.

3 The doctor _____ Tim's appendix _____ yesterday.

4 Tim _____ to work after only five days.

5 Yesterday a group of visitors arrived and Rebecca _____ them.

6 When she was in Italy Julia _____ a lot.

7 The next day Tim _____ Julia at seven o'clock, but she wasn't in.

3

Here are some more people that Tim is going to interview. What have they done? Use these expressions.

live in a tree for a year
climb Mount Everest
visit every country in the world
win the lottery
walk to the North Pole
build their own house
fly across Africa in a balloon
sail round Australia

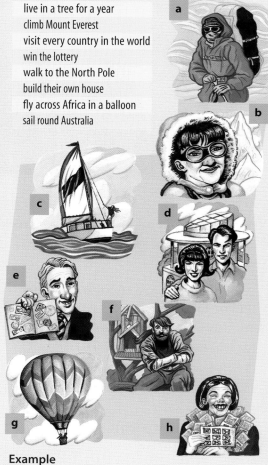

Example

He has walked to the North Pole.

4a

Have you ever done these things?

1   live in another country
2   be to another country for a holiday
3   have appendicitis
4   be in hospital
5   appear on TV
6   do anything unusual
7   win anything
8   play a joke on someone
9   want to get away from it all
10 have a strange dream

Example

I have / haven't lived in another country.

4b

Work with a partner. Interview him / her. If he / she has done it, find out some more details.

Example

Have you ever lived in another country?

Yes, I have.

Where did you live?

I lived in the USA.

How long were you there?

About six months.

Did you enjoy it?

Yes. I had a great time.

5a

What can you remember about the people in the video? Work in a group of three. Choose two of the characters. Write down six things that you know about them. Try to use the the Present simple tense, the Past simple tense and the Present perfect.

5b

Compare your ideas with a partner.

6a

Look at the underlined words and expressions. These are fillers. They don't add a lot to the meaning, but they make the conversation smoother and more informal. What fillers do you have in your own language?

1

A: *So, shall we try, you know, that new restaurant near the station?*

B: *Well, I've heard it isn't very good. In fact Ted said it was pretty awful. And it was a bit expensive, too.*

A: *Oh, I see.*

2

A: *Are you all right?*

B: *Yes, I've just got a bit of a headache, that's all.*

A: *Well, I think you should be in bed.*

6b

Work with a partner. Read these dialogues. Add fillers where possible.

1

A: *What shall we do this evening?*

B: *Why don't we go to the cinema? We can see that new Spielberg film.*

A: *No, I'd prefer to get a video.*

B: *Why?*

A: *I don't want to go out. I feel tired.*

2

A: *Did you enjoy the conference?*

B: *Yes, it was good. Some of the sessions were great.*

A: *That's good.*

B: *Why didn't Martha go?*

A: *She was too busy.*

Role play

Work in a group of three. Write and act a play to fit this scenario.

Student A, Student B and Student C all work in the same office. Student A fancies Student B and thinks that Student B feels the same way about him / her.

Student A wants to ask Student B out, but every time he / she tries Student C interrupts. Eventually Student A asks Student B, but when they go out together, they meet Student C and he / she wants to go with them.

57

Language in use

1a Making arrangements

Match the halves of the sentences.

1	Would you like to	a	meet at the restaurant?
2	Yes, I'd	b	that new restaurant?
3	Shall we try	c	any good for you?
4	That would	d	call for you at about seven?
5	Is this evening	e	you.
6	Yes, it's	f	be nice.
7	Shall I	g	love to.
8	Can we	h	go out for a meal sometime?
9	OK. See you	i	there at, say, 7.30.
10	Yes. See	j	fine.

1b

Make new dialogues for these situations.

1

A: Suggest

B: Accept. Ask when.

A: Suggest tomorrow.

B: Accept. Ask what time.

A: You can call for B at

B: You'd prefer to meet at the cinema at

A: Agree.

2

A: Suggest

B: Accept.
Suggest the café in the Square.

A: Accept. Suggest Thursday evening.

B: Thursday's no good for you. You're going to be away on Thursday and Friday.

A: Suggest Saturday.

B: Accept. Suggest that you meet at the café at

A: You can call for B at

B: Accept.

2 the

Some of the expressions in these sentences don't need *the*. Delete it where necessary.

Example

1   The doctor says I can go back to the work next week.

2   Tim was in the hospital for three days.

3   Julia took him to the doctor.

4   I can go the home tomorrow.

5   Gary had the appendicitis when he was at the school.

6   Tim and Julia met Gary at the restaurant.

7   I have to go to the work early tomorrow.

8   What time do you usually start the work?

9   Shall we go to that restaurant near the hospital?

10   I must go to the bank.

11   I travelled around a bit after I left the university.

12   Is Rebecca at the home?

3 Useful expressions

Complete the dialogues with the expressions.

say
Can I join you
Me, too
He's on the phone
Oh, I see
I've got an early start in the morning
it was great fun
A couple of hours
Sure
Is everything OK?
you two
if you want to
I'm just a bit tired
the best thing is

1

A: Well, I'd better be off.   .

B: . See you tomorrow.

2

A: Hello,   . Are you going to the pub?

B: Yes, we are.

A: ?

B: .

3

A: Is Frederick in? I need to have a word with him.

B: , but you can wait,   .

4

A: Did you enjoy the party?

B: Yes,   .

5

A: Did you get the job?

B: Yes, I did and   I can start on Monday.

6

A: You don't look well.   ?

B: Yes,   . I had an early start this morning.

A:

7

A: How long is this meeting going to be?

B: probably.

A: Well, can we start a bit earlier at,   , 2.15?

Grammar summary

going to

To talk about future plans we use the Present simple tense of *to be* + *going to* + the stem form of the verb.

Positive statements

I	'm (am)		catch a train.
He She It	's (is)	going to	interview a teacher. start work.
We You They	're (are)		

Negative statements

I	'm not (am not)		start now.
He She It	isn't (is not)	going to	work tomorrow. finish in time.
We You They	aren't (are not)		

Questions

Am	I		
Is	he she it	going to	have dinner with Julia? visit Tim in hospital?
Are	we you they		

Short answers

Yes,	I am. he is. she is.	No,	I'm not. he isn't. she isn't.

The Present perfect tense – regular and irregular verbs

We make the Present perfect with the verb *have* and a past participle. Verbs that are regular in the Past simple tense are also regular in the Present perfect. The spelling rules for past participles are the same as for the Past simple tense (see p43). Verbs that are irregular in the Past simple tense also have an irregular past participle.

Present perfect: *I've seen that film.*
Past simple: *I saw it yesterday.*

Positive statements

I We You They	've (have)	worked in advertising. lived in Italy. won the lottery.
He She It	's (has)	

Negative statements

I We You They	haven't (have not)	had appendicitis. lived abroad. been to Paris.
He She It	hasn't (has not)	

Questions

Have	I we you they	lived abroad? been to Paris?
Has	he she it	

Short answers

Yes,	I have. you have. we have.	No,	I haven't. you haven't. we haven't.

The Present perfect tense and the Past simple tense

We use the Present perfect to talk about our experiences, and when the time is either not known or not important. We use the Past simple tense when the time is given and / or it is important.
I've done some scuba-diving. (We don't know when.)
I did it in 1998. (The time is important.)

Phrasal verbs

When people are speaking they often use phrasal verbs in place of more formal verbs.
The doctor removed his appendix.
The doctor took out his appendix.
He returned to work last Tuesday.
He went back to work last Tuesday.

Some phrasal verbs can be separated by the object.
Tim switched off the TV.
Tim switched the TV off.

Some phrasal verbs cannot be separated.
She is looking after the visitors.
Would you like to go out for dinner?

59

EPISODE 1

GARY: *Good morning. It's seven thirty. I'm Gary Fenton. Here is the news. The Prime Minister is in the United States today for talks with the American president at the Whitehouse. The talks are very important for British and American …*

SANDRA: *Look at the time. Julia! It's half past seven. Your train's at quarter to eight.*

JULIA: *Coming. Is this OK?*

SANDRA: *Lovely, dear. Well, good luck.*

JULIA: *Thanks, Mum. Bye, Dad.*

COLIN: *Bye, love.*

SANDRA: *Colin. It's her first day today.*

COLIN: *What? Oh yes.*

JULIA: *Thanks, Dad. Bye.*

DRIVER: *That's £4.50, please.*

JULIA: *Here you are.*

DRIVER: *Thank you very much, thank you.*

TIM: *OK, bye. Bye. Excuse me.*

JULIA: *Sorry.*

TIM: *Morning, Ted.*

TED: *Good morning, Tim. How are you?*

TIM: *I'm fine, thanks. And you?*

TED: *Good morning. Can I help you?*

JULIA: *Yes, Martha McKay, please. She's the producer.*

TED: *That's 5894 … What's your name, please?*

JULIA: *Julia Drake.*

TED: *Hello. Miss Drake is at Reception … Yes, all right.*

DOORMAN: *Mrs McKay is in Room 12. That's on the second floor. The lift is over there.*

JULIA: *Thank you.*

REBECCA: *And what's your address? … 94 Tindall Street. How do you spell Tindall, please? … T I N D A double L. Thank you. And your postcode? … Can you repeat that, please?*

KT9 8NB. And your telephone number? 01372 89531. Thank you, Ms Fossett. Goodbye.

JULIA: *Hello. I'm …*

MARTHA: *Julia! Welcome to Apex TV. Come in … No, don't come in. This is my personal assistant, Rebecca Bond.*

JULIA: *How do you do, Rebecca.*

REBECCA: *Pleased to meet you.*

MARTHA: *Come and meet some of the people in the newsroom. Is Frederick in? He's the Managing Director.*

REBECCA: *No. He's in London.*

MARTHA: *Oh, I see. Right. Well. Come on then, Julia. That's Tim Barnes over there. He's a reporter. Tim, this is Julia. She's our new trainee.*

TIM: *Hi.*

JULIA: *Hi.*

TIM: *This is a very interesting story, Martha. Look at this.*

MARTHA: *Tell me about it this afternoon. OK?*

TIM: *Sure. See you around, Julie.*

JULIA: *Julia.*

TIM: *Sorry?*

JULIA: *My name isn't Julie. It's Julia.*

TIM: *Oh, right.*

JULIA: *And address has got two Ds.*

TIM: *What?*

JULIA: *Address is A, double D.*

TIM: *Right. Thank you.*

JULIA: *Don't mention it.*

GARY: *Who's that young woman with Martha and Sean?*

TIM: *Her name's Julia. She's a new trainee.*

GARY: *Mmm. She's very pretty.*

MARTHA: *Well, that's everyone, I think. Tea or coffee?*

JULIA: *Coffee, please.*

MARTHA: *Black or white?*

JULIA: *Oh, white with no sugar, please.*

GARY: *Hello. You're Julia, aren't*

you?

JULIA: *Yes, and …*

GARY: *Pleased to meet you. I'm Gary.*

JULIA: *Nice to meet you, Gary. What do you do?*

GARY: *I'm a newsreader.*

JULIA: *Oh yes! You're Gary Fenton. You're my Mum's favourite newsreader.*

MARTHA: *Here you are. Hello, Gary. This is Julia.*

GARY: *Er, yes, I know. Anyway, I must be off.*

JULIA: *He's very nice.*

MARTHA: *Yes.*

JULIA: *Hi. I'm home.*

SANDRA: *Hello, dear. How's your new job? Tell me all about it.*

JULIA: *It's great. Everyone's very friendly. Well, almost everyone.*

EPISODE 2

TIM: *No, I can't make it today, Ellie … I haven't got time. I have to finish this programme and … Ellie? Ellie!*

JULIA: *Hi, Tim. Good morning, Julia. How nice to see you.*

REBECCA: *Martha, can we take a look at the diary for this week?*

MARTHA: *Now? Oh, yes, all right.*

REBECCA: *Well, this morning you're on the food programme. Then this afternoon you've got a meeting with Floyd and Hank. That's at quarter to two. Then tomorrow you've got an appointment at the dentist's in the morning at quarter past ten.*

MARTHA: *Marvellous!*

REBECCA: *Then in the afternoon you've got a meeting with Frederick. Oh no, sorry. He can't make it. He had to go to Paris.*

MARTHA: *So is Tuesday afternoon free now?*

REBECCA: *No, you have to finish the Videocom report – oh, hi, Julia – then on Wednesday morning you're at the Birmingham conference.*

TIM: *Martha. Can I have a word?*

MARTHA: *Yes, Tim. What is it?*

TIM: *I haven't got an assistant for this afternoon for the story about Carl Stalker. You know – the windows guy.*

MARTHA: *Oh yes. Well who have we got? Ah, Chloe's away. Gita's on holiday …*

TIM: *And everybody else is busy. But I have to have an assistant.*

JULIA: *Can I do it? Can I be your assistant, Tim?*

MARTHA: *That's an idea.*
TIM: *She hasn't got the experience, Martha.*
MARTHA: *She has to learn.*
JULIA: *And there's nobody else.*
TIM: *OK.*
MARTHA: *See you later.*
JULIA: *So what's this job about? 'Wonderful Windows. Can you believe it? New windows for just £500.' … And who's this guy Walker?*
TIM: *Stalker. Carl Stalker. He's the Managing Director of Wonderful Windows. And he's got his customers' money but they haven't got their windows. These are all letters from his customers. We have to leave at one thirty sharp.*

SEAN: *Jason's in trouble at school again.*
JULIA: *Who's Jason?*
SEAN: *He's my son.*
JULIA: *Oh, how many children have you got?*
SEAN: *Two – a son and a daughter.*
JULIA: *What's your daughter's name?*
SEAN: *Kylie. She's 13. Jason's 16. My wife Sharon …*
TIM: *OK Julia. Now you wait at the corner with one of these. Stalker's got a blue Jaguar.*
JULIA: *What does he look like?*
TIM: *He's quite tall. He's got short, dark hair. When you see him, call me.*

JULIA: *Tim. Tim. Here he is. A blue Jaguar and … Oh no. It isn't him. It's a woman. And it isn't a Jaguar. Sorry. Wait. Yes. He's here. A blue Jag registration number S307 ABW.*
TIM: *Great. OK. Get ready, Sean. Mr Stalker. I'm from Apex TV. Can I ask you some questions?*
STALKER: *What the …? No, you can't.*
TIM: *Where is your customers' money, Mr Stalker?*
STALKER: *I've got nothing to say.*
TIM: *Mr Stalker. You and your wife have got a big house and an expensive car, but your customers have got nothing. Where is their money, Mr Stalker?*
STALKER: *Look. Go away and switch that thing off.*
TIM: *Where's the money, Mr Stalker?*
STALKER: *Clear off!*
JULIA: *Are you all right, Sean?*
TIM: *Great. We've got him now. How about a drink? Oh, just a*

minute. *What's the time?*
JULIA: *It's half past seven.*
TIM: *Excuse me.*

ELLIE: *If that's Tim, I'm not here.*
REBECCA: *Hello?*
TIM: *Hi, Rebecca. It's Tim.*
REBECCA: *Hi Tim. Erm, Ellie's not here.*
TIM: *Oh, well, can you video the football match for me? I can't get back in time.*
REBECCA: *Yes, OK.*
TIM: *Thanks, Rebecca. See you later.*
REBECCA: *Yes. Bye, Tim. Ellie!*

JULIA: *Is Rebecca still at work?*
TIM: *No, she's at home.*
JULIA: *Oh, are you and Rebecca …*
SEAN: *See you at the usual place.*
TIM: *Yes. See you there. Sorry. Are Rebecca and I …?*
JULIA: *Oh, nothing. Let's go.*

EPISODE 3

REBECCA: *Rebecca Bond speaking.*
GARY: *Good morning. This is Angus Moon from The Modern Woman magazine. We'd like to do an article on the job of a personal assistant.*
REBECCA: *Uh huh.*
GARY: *Martha McKay's an old friend of mine and she says that you are a wonderful PA. Are you busy now? Can I ask you a few questions?*
REBECCA: *Well, yes, of course.*
GARY: *Great. First a few questions about you. What time do you get up in the morning?*
REBECCA: *I always get up at seven o'clock. I have a shower and wash my hair. I have breakfast at half past seven. Then I get dressed …*
GARY: *And what do you normally have for breakfast?*
REBECCA: *Breakfast? Oh, I usually have a glass of orange juice, a grapefruit, two slices of toast – one with butter and jam, and one with butter and marmalade. And two cups of coffee.*
GARY: *You're very organized.*
REBECCA: *Well, you have to be for this job.*
GARY: *And what do you do in your free time?*
REBECCA: *I go to the gym three times a week – on Monday, Wednesday, and Saturday. On Thursday evening I go to my dance class …*
GARY: *Oh, do you like dancing?*

REBECCA: *Yes, I do. I like cooking, too. And I love going to parties.*
GARY: *OK, Rebecca. Thank you very much.*
REBECCA: *But don't you want to talk about my job?*
GARY: *Well, I have got one last question. Um, do you know Gary Fenton?*
REBECCA: *Gary? Yes, of course. He's one of our newsreaders …*
GARY: *And he's a very good newsreader, isn't he?*
REBECCA: *Gary! You …*
GARY: *Hey. It's only a joke, Rebecca.*
REBECCA: *Well, I don't think it's funny.*

MARTHA: *Now, I always come on at the end of the programme and try the food and drinks. That's the next thing. Is everything ready?*
JULIA: *Yes, I think so.*
REBECCA: *Frederick's on the phone, Martha. He's in New York.*
MARTHA: *OK. Five minutes then, Julia.*
JULIA: *Five minutes, Neil.*

GARY: *Some salt in the lemonade. And some chilli powder in the soup.*
JULIA: *Hello, Gary. Do you want to try it?*
GARY: *Oh no. Martha always tries the food and drinks. But, um, can I watch?*
MARTHA: *If you want to.*
JULIA: *Ready, Martha? OK.*

MARTHA: *So, this is our lunch for a warm summer's day – a green salad, cheese with French bread, cold tomato and onion soup, and home-made lemonade. It's time to try it. No. Why don't we make a change today? Here in the studio today is everybody's favourite newsreader, Gary Fenton. Would you like to try this delicious meal, Gary? I bet you can't wait to taste it. Here. Try the home-made lemonade first. Isn't that wonderful, Gary?*
GARY: *Very nice.*
MARTHA: *Now, what about this soup? A nice cold soup, eh Gary? Come on, a big spoonful. Well, that's it for this week. I hope you enjoy your summer lunch as much as Gary. Bye.*

GARY: *OK. What would you like?*
REBECCA: *I'll have a glass of white wine, please*
JULIA: *Me, too.*

61

TIM: *Home-made lemonade for me, please, Gary.*

GARY: *Very funny.*

REBECCA: *Just a joke, Gary. Just a joke.*

TIM: *I'll have a mineral water. I have to drive.*

GARY: *Ice and lemon?*

TIM: *Yes, please. Oh, I must give Ellie a ring.*

GARY: *Two glasses of white wine, a mineral water with ice and lemon and a pint of lager …*

JULIA: *Who's Ellie?*

REBECCA: *Tim's girlfriend.*

JULIA: *Oh! Aren't you Tim's girlfriend?*

REBECCA: *Me? No. Ellie's my flatmate. Tim lives upstairs.*

JULIA: *Oh, I see. What does she do?*

REBECCA: *She works in a hotel, so she works funny hours.*

GARY: *Here we are. Nice, cold drinks.*

TIM: *No reply.*

EPISODE 4

TED: *Morning, Tim.*

TIM: *Morning, Ted.*

TED: *Oh dear. You look tired. What time were you up this morning?*

TIM: *About four o'clock. There was an accident at the station. There weren't any trains for five hours.*

TED: *Terrible.*

TIM: *Oh hi, Rebecca.*

REBECCA: *Hi. Thanks Ted. What's the date today, Tim?*

TIM: *What?*

REBECCA: *Today's date. What is it?*

TIM: *Er, it's the fourth of October.*

REBECCA: *And what do you know about the fourth of October?*

TIM: *It's the day after the third of October?*

REBECCA: *Try again, Tim. Think of your girlfriend.*

TIM: *Oh no! It's Ellie's birthday. But I haven't got her a card or a present or anything. Excuse me …*

JULIA: *Oh, sorry!*

REBECCA: *Good afternoon, Julia.*

JULIA: *I know. I'm sorry. The trains were all late.*

TED: *There was an accident at the station.*

JULIA: *Is Martha annoyed?*

REBECCA: *Well, she isn't pleased. This is the second time this week.*

JULIA: *Yes, but it wasn't my fault today.*

REBECCA: *And you were late last Thursday, too.*

JULIA: *Well, that's it. I must find a flat in town.*

REBECCA: *Are there any places in there?*

JULIA: *No, there aren't.*

REBECCA: *What about this? Second floor flat – bedroom, living room, small kitchen and bathroom / WC.*

JULIA: *Yes, but it's £600 a month. I can't afford that.*

REBECCA: *No, I suppose not. You could try an agency.*

JULIA: *I haven't got time.*

REBECCA: *Ask Martha for some time off this afternoon.*

JULIA: *Oh come on, Rebecca. I was late this morning, remember?*

REBECCA: *Well, try it. Martha's got a teleconference with Frederick all afternoon.*

JULIA: *A teleconference?*

REBECCA: *Yes. Frederick's in Tokyo.*

JULIA: *Oh, so Martha doesn't need me.*

JULIA: *So let me see. There's the room and the kitchen, and the bathroom and the toilet are in the hall.*

MR JACKSON: *Yes, that's right. You share them with the people upstairs. They're very nice people.*

JULIA: *And how much is it, Mr Jackson?*

MR JACKSON: *It's only £65 a week. So are you interested?*

JULIA: *Yes, definitely. The people upstairs?*

MR JACKSON: *Uh, yes.*

TED: *Reception.*

GARY: *Any luck?*

JULIA: *No. There isn't anything. Everything's too far away, too expensive, too noisy, or just grotty.*

REBECCA: *Never mind. Look. Come to my place for a drink. It's a sort of surprise for Ellie's birthday.*

JULIA: *OK.*

TIM: *Back in a minute.*

JULIA: *This is a nice place, Rebecca.*

REBECCA: *Yes, I like it. This is Ellie's room. We've got this living room, a kitchen, and the bathroom's down the hall, next to my bedroom.*

JULIA: *Where do you live, Gary?*

GARY: *I've got a flat just round the corner.*

REBECCA: *Gary's got a lovely place. It's on the sixth floor and it's got a great view. Tea, everyone?*

GARY: *There's a message on your answerphone.*

TIM: *Happy birthday to you. Happy birthday to you. Happy birthday, dear Ellie. Happy birthday to you. See you later. Love you. Bye.*

GARY: *Love you. Bye. You old romantic.*

JULIA: *Well, I think it's very sweet, Tim.*

ELLIE: *Hi, Rebecca. It's me …*

REBECCA: *Sshh, everybody. It's Ellie.*

ELLIE: *Hi, Rebecca. It's me, Ellie. This is just to say goodbye. I'm really sorry about this, but I've got a job in a hotel in San Francisco, and so … well … er … The rent for this month is on the dressing table in my room. There's a letter for Tim there, too. Can you give it to him, please? So, er … that's it. Bye. Take care.*

JULIA: *Oh dear. Poor Tim.*

REBECCA: *Well, it was very strange. I mean she wasn't here last night and then she wasn't here this morning and …*

GARY: *Look on the bright side. You need a new flatmate now. Julia needs a room, so …*

JULIA: *Gary!*

REBECCA: *It's all right, Julia. Gary's right. The room is yours, if you want it.*

JULIA: *What? Really?*

REBECCA: *Yes, really.*

JULIA: *Oh, thank you! That's great. Wonderful! Oh, Tim. I'm sorry.*

EPISODE 5

SEAN: *I'm sorry I'm late, Tim. I had to go to the police station about Kylie and Jason. They …*

TIM: *Not now, Sean. We need to go in five minutes.*

SEAN: *What's the matter with him today?*

REBECCA: *It's Ellie.*

SEAN: *Ellie?*

REBECCA: *She's gone.*

SEAN: *Gone?*

REBECCA: *To the States.*

SEAN: *To the States?*

REBECCA: *She left yesterday. You see, yesterday was Ellie's birthday. Tim, Gary, Julia and I went back to my place for a birthday drink for Ellie. Ellie wasn't there, but there was a* message from her on the answerphone. She said that she had a new job in San Francisco and well ... goodbye.

SEAN: *What did Tim do?*

REBECCA: *He just walked out of the flat. He didn't say a word. It was all very sad and, well, embarrassing. We didn't know what to do.*

SEAN: *No wonder he's in a bad mood.*

REBECCA: *But it's not all bad news, because Julia's my new flatmate now.*

TIM: *Come on, Sean. We haven't got all day.*

REBECCA: *Have a nice day.*

COLIN: *There, that's the lot.*

REBECCA: *Cup of tea, Mr Drake?*

COLIN: *Um, no, thank you, Rebecca. I'd better be off now.*

JULIA: *Thanks, Dad.*

COLIN: *Don't mention it, love.*

JULIA: *Bye.*

COLIN: *Bye.*

REBECCA: *Bye.*

COLIN: *Bye Rebecca.*

REBECCA: *Welcome to Wellington Gardens.*

JULIA: *I still can't believe it.*

REBECCA: *Why don't we have a party – a sort of 'Welcome to Julia' thing?*

JULIA: *Oh, yes. Great idea. When?*

REBECCA: *Next Friday? We can invite some of the neighbours and everyone from work.*

JULIA: *Everyone? Even Frederick?*

REBECCA: *Don't worry. He's in South Africa for the rest of the week.*

JULIA: *So who can we invite?*

SEAN: *Oh, what's this?*

JULIA: *It's an invitation to our party.*

SEAN: *A party, eh? When is it?*

JULIA: *It's next Friday. The eighteenth. Tim, here.*

SEAN: *Great! I like parties.*

TIM: *We can't come.*

SEAN: *But ...*

TIM: *We've got that programme to finish.*

SEAN: *Can't we do it another time? It's Julia's ...*

TIM: *No!*

JULIA: *Oh, well ...*

GARY: *Hi, Tim. It's party time.*

TIM: *No, it isn't. OK. I think we can take a look at that now. Last year Richard Bennett gave up his job in a London bank and decided to walk to the South Pole. Why did you give up your job, Richard?*

RICHARD: *Well, I didn't like my job*

and I had a lot of problems at home. I just wanted to get away from it all. I wanted to find myself, if you like.

TIM: *So you left England in August. What did you do first?*

RICHARD: *I flew to Buenos Aires in Argentina. From there I travelled to the Antarctic by boat.*

TIM: *When did you actually start your journey to the Pole?*

RICHARD: *Well, I had to wait for a few weeks, because the weather was very bad, so I didn't set off until the end of September.*

TIM: *Did anyone go with you?*

RICHARD: *No, I was on my own.*

TIM: *And did you reach the South Pole?*

RICHARD: *No, I didn't. After about three hundred kilometres I fell into a huge crevasse – you know – a big hole – about ten metres deep.*

TIM: *Were you hurt?*

RICHARD: *Yes, I broke my arm. I couldn't climb out.*

TIM: *What did you do?*

RICHARD: *Well, fortunately, my sledge fell into the hole with me, so I had food, and I had my radio, too. And I called for help.*

TIM: *How long were you there before they found you?*

RICHARD: *Five days. There was a bad storm, you see. I thought it was the end, but then suddenly I heard voices and dogs. I shouted and shouted and faces appeared above me.*

TIM: *What did you think about, while you were in the crevasse?*

RICHARD: *I thought about my life back in England. And the funny thing was that all my problems at home and at work weren't important any more. I just wanted to be with my family and friends again. Life's very short, you know. You have to enjoy it while you can.*

TIM: *Thank you very much.*

SEAN: *Can I just look at that last part again?*

RICHARD: *I thought about my life back in England. And the funny thing was that all my problems at home and at work weren't important any more. I just wanted to be with my family and friends again. Life's very short, you know. You have to enjoy it while you can.*

TIM: *Thank you very much.*

SEAN: *Yes, that's fine. Do you want a cup of coffee? Tim?*

TIM: *Sorry. What did you say?*

SEAN: *Would you like a coffee?*

TIM: *No thanks, Sean. We've got a party to go to.*

EPISODE 6

JULIA: *What do you think, Rebecca? The skirt or the trousers? I can't afford both.*

REBECCA: *Hmm. I don't know. How much are they?*

JULIA: *The skirt's £28.50. The trousers are a bit more expensive, but not much ...*

JULIA: *Look. There's Gary.*

REBECCA: *Where?*

JULIA: *There. He's going into the Men's department.*

REBECCA: *Oh, I suppose he's buying some new clothes for his interview with that magazine.*

JULIA: *Oh yes. What did he say? The readers of Stars and Style magazine voted me the best-dressed newsreader on TV. Let's see what he's buying.*

JULIA: *Hi, Gary. What are you doing?*

GARY: *I'm looking for a shirt and a tie to go with my new suit.*

JULIA: *Are they for your interview?*

GARY: *Oh, do you know about that?*

JULIA: *Oh, come on, Gary. Everybody knows. You mention it at least ten times a day.*

GARY: *Excuse me. Can I try these on, please?*

ASSISTANT: *Sure. The changing rooms are over there.*

GARY: *Thank you.*

REBECCA: *How many shirts are you taking?*

GARY: *Only the best is good enough for the best-dressed newsreader.*

GARY: *Hi, Tim.*

TIM: *OK, Gary. What's in the bags?*

GARY: *Oh, these? It's my new suit and things for my interview about ...*

TIM AND GARY: *... the best dressed newsreader.*

TIM: *Yes, we know. Armani, eh? Bet that cost a bit.*

GARY: *Well, if it's good, the price doesn't matter.*

TIM: *Did you hear that?*

JULIA: *Yes, he's even worse than usual.*

TIM: *Somebody should do something about him. When is this interview anyway?*

REBECCA: *Straight after the six o'clock news.*

GARY: *Psst! Sean! Sean!*

VOICE: *Gary Fenton to the studio, please. Five minutes.*

MARTHA: *Oh there you are, Gary. Why are you so late?*

GARY: *Good evening. This is Gary Fenton with the six o'clock news.*

MARTHA: *Gary, your visitors.*

CHARLOTTE: *Charlotte Mortimer from Stars and Style magazine. Pleased to meet you, Mr Fenton, or may I call you Gary?*

GARY: *Of course.*

CHARLOTTE: *Now, can we take some photographs first? Oh no. We always see you at your desk, Gary.*

GARY: *Well, I feel more comfortable here.*

CHARLOTTE: *But I'm sure all our readers want to know if you've got any legs.*

GARY: *I'd really prefer to be at my desk.*

CHARLOTTE: *Come on now, Gary. Don't be shy …*

GARY: *All right!*

CHARLOTTE: *What are you wearing? Er, well, perhaps at the desk is better.*

JULIA: *What's happening?*

REBECCA: *The reporter's interviewing Gary.*

TIM: *And Gary always enjoys interviews.*

REBECCA: *Well, he isn't enjoying this one. I think we should give his trousers back now.*

TIM: *Why? … Oh, all right.*

CHARLOTTE: *So when did you start doing that?*

GARY: *A couple of years ago.*

TIM: *Sorry to interrupt. We found these, Gary.*

GARY: *Excuse me. Photograph?*

JULIA: *Come on, Gary. Cheer up. The magazine got photos of you in your new suit in the end.*

REBECCA: *But you looked so funny in those baggy old trousers.*

TIM: *Where did you get them, anyway?*

GARY: *They were Sean's Oh no, Sean!*

EPISODE 7

SEAN: *So what are we going to do at this school?*

JULIA: *Tim's going to interview one of the teachers. She's won the lottery twice.*

SEAN: *I've never won the lottery.*

In fact, I've never won anything!

JULIA: *Is everything OK?*

TIM: *Sure. Let's go. Oh!*

JULIA: *Tim! Are you all right?*

TIM: *Yes, I'm fine. I've just got stomach-ache, that's all.*

JULIA: *You can't work like this. You should be at home in bed.*

TIM: *Look. I've never missed a day's work in my life and I'm not going to start now. Anyway, who's going to do the interview if I'm not there?*

JULIA: *Me.*

TIM: *Have you ever done an interview before?*

JULIA: *No, I haven't, but I've watched you several times and Sean's here. He's filmed hundreds of interviews.*

TIM: *No, it's OK, I can … Ow ah!*

JULIA: *Give me your car keys. I'm going to take you straight to the doctor.*

JULIA: *Hi, how are you?*

TIM: *Hi, Julia. Did you get the interview all right?*

JULIA: *Yes, everything was fine. But what about you?*

TIM: *I feel a bit sore. They took my appendix out yesterday afternoon.*

JULIA: *I know. I came to see you, but you were asleep … I was with Rebecca.*

TIM: *Uh-huh. I've never been in hospital before.*

JULIA: *How long are you going to be in here?*

TIM: *I can go home tomorrow and the doctor says I can go back to work next week, if I want to.*

JULIA: *Tim. Don't you ever stop?*

TIM: *Hi, Gary.*

GARY: *Tim … Oh, hello, Julia. Appendicitis, eh? Ah no, I suppose you can't eat anything at the moment. Julia?*

JULIA: *No thanks.*

GARY: *I've had appendicitis, you know. Have you, Julia? Very painful. Now when did I have it? Oh yes. I was at school. It must be oh, twenty years ago.*

MARTHA: *Hello Tim. What did the doctor say?*

TIM: *All clear. And the best thing is I can eat normally again.*

MARTHA: *Good.*

TIM: *Er, Julia … I, em, wanted to say thank you for all your help when, you know … and well, erm, would you like to go out for a meal sometime, just to, you know, say thank you …*

JULIA: *Yes, I'd love to.*

TIM: *Shall we try that new Italian place near the museum?*

JULIA: *Mmm. That would be nice. When?*

TIM: *Is this evening any good for you?*

JULIA: *Yes, it's fine.*

TIM: *Great. Shall I call for you about eight?*

JULIA: *I'm going to be in town anyway. So can we meet at the restaurant at say half past seven?*

TIM: *OK. Tim Barnes. Hi Pete …*

JULIA: *Mmm. This is good. I love Italian food.*

TIM: *Have you ever been to Italy?*

JULIA: *I lived there for a couple of years.*

TIM: *Really?*

JULIA: *It was after I left university. I worked in a travel company. You know, looking after groups of British tourists.*

TIM: *Did you enjoy it?*

JULIA: *Yes, it was great fun. I like travelling. What about you?*

TIM: *I've travelled around a bit – mostly in Asia and South America, but I've never actually lived in another country. Em … You've got some sauce on your cheek.*

JULIA: *Have I? Where?*

GARY: *Hi, you two.*

JULIA: *Oh, hello, Gary.*

GARY: *Can I join you? I'm having dinner here, too, but my friends aren't here yet … You've got a bit of sauce on your cheek, Julia.*

JULIA: *Thank you, Gary. I can do it.*

JULIA: *That was a really good meal. I enjoyed it.*

TIM: *Yes, me too. Until Gary arrived.*

JULIA: *Yes.*

TIM: *Um, well, I've got an early start tomorrow.*

JULIA: *Yes.*

TIM: *So …*

JULIA: *Yes. Goodnight.*

TIM: *Goodnight. See you tomorrow.*

JULIA: *Tim!*

TIM: *Yes?*

JULIA: *I can't find my keys, I think I've left them at work.*

TIM: *Oh. Isn't Rebecca in?*

JULIA: *I don't know. Probably not.*

TIM: *Oh dear.*

REBECCA: *Oh hi, hi Tim. I heard voices. I'm just on the phone to my sister so I'll see you in a minute.*

TIM: *Still locked out?*

JULIA: *Yes.*